Contents

11 OTHER FORMS OF AUDIO DRAMA AND ITS FUTURE154

Preface

AMDG was the dedication we put at the beginning of our school homework. It stands for *Ad Maiorem Dei Gloriam*: To The Greater Glory Of God. I have to thank the Jesuits for my love of literature and of the spoken word.

I should also like to dedicate this book to two women: my late, heroic mother, a one time successful novelist and journalist, whose subsequent rejection slips could have papered the entire walls of the cottage, where I was brought up; and Jane, my humorous, loyal wife who has put up with my vagaries for over 30 years. As our friend, Enyd Williams observed: 'Shaun is the Catholic and Jane is the Saint'.

I should also like to thank a multitude of writers, actors, composers, musicians, technicians, production assistants, students and fellow producers, who have helped to make my working life, as a radio Drama producer, a joy and an inspiration. Many will be mentioned in these pages. In this third edition I should like to thank Tom Bennett for his research into Internet Drama sites and his untiring work on our website, www.soundplay.co.uk. I am grateful to my friends - John Tydeman, ex Head of BBC Radio Drama, Jonathan Smith, playwright, novelist and schoolmaster and Badria Timimi, drama student, for reading my manuscript and for their helpful and encouraging comments.

I should particularly like to honour the memory of the late Richard Imison, BBC Script Editor Radio Drama for over twenty years, whose perfectionism, creative intelligence and encouragement to writers helped Radio Drama to remain a considerable art form from the 1960s to the 1980s.

Finally I should like to thank the listeners, the audience without whom audio drama would not exist. It is not surprising that a high proportion of listeners and of radio playwrights are women. They are generally better listeners than men. I hope the reader will bear this in mind when from time to time I use the personal pronoun: 'he'.

Shaun MacLoughlin

1 Understanding Why Radio is Different

Comparing Radio with other Media Forms

Radio Drama has been described variously as the 'Mind as Stage', 'The Theatre Between The Ears', 'The Theatre Where Anything That Can Be Imagined Can Happen' and 'The Auditorium of the Cranium.'. The last phrase is ugly, but apt. In the early 1970's the Germans invented a stereophonic microphone that they called a *kunstkopf* (literally an 'art-head'). It was constructed in the shape of a skull to capture sound as we actually receive it. BBC producers used to sit around with earphones, listening to recordings of a pin being dropped under a jet aircraft taking off at Tempelhof Airport, Berlin. The *kunstkopf* bore a remarkable resemblance to the then Head of BBC Radio Drama, Martin Esslin.

However radio drama is really about something more ancient and wonderful: 'In the beginning was the word.' It is primarily about the power and the beauty of the spoken word, which can convey to the human imagination anything of which it can conceive.

There is the mythical small boy, who prefers radio to TV because the pictures are better and the colours more vivid. In *The Hitch-hiker's Guide to the Galaxy* twenty-six men can fit inside a sardine tin. In 1938 the comedian Arthur Askey declared: 'Radio is the only medium where a man can sit on a circular saw in outer space.' It is a medium for an audience with an active imagination. It is for listeners who like to participate and to contribute something from their rich and reflective experience of life. It is a medium that 'stimulates' the imagination, unlike TV which only 'satisfies' it.

Painting our own pictures

I should love to be a voyeur and see the pictures, being formed inside the head of each listener to the following excerpt from Douglas Adams' marvellously inventive *The Hitch-Hiker's Guide to the Galaxy*. We, each of us, bring something different to it. Our picture of the characters speaking will gradually take shape and our picture of the man with five heads, of the wall, of the motion of Southend's sea front and of the colour of the sea, will vary from listener to listener. From the dialogue and the actors' performances and from our differing experience of life, we shall, each of us, conjure up our own characters.

FORD: Perhaps we'd better ask somebody what's
                  going on?
                  How about that man over there?

ARTHUR: The one with five heads creeping up the wall?

FORD: Er - yes (ONLY A SUSPICION OF A DOUBT
                  IN HIS VOICE)

ARTHUR: Sir, excuse me, er - excuse me –

FX: WILD TRUMPETING AND BELLOWING LIKE AN
          ELEPHANT OR SOMETHING

ARTHUR: You know, if this is Southend, there's
                  something very odd about it.

FORD: You mean the way the sea stays steady as a
                  rock and the buildings keep washing up and
                  down? Yes, *I* thought that was odd -

I am going to give many illustrations from radio plays. I strongly recommend, you read them aloud to yourself or better still with your friends, fellow students or families. This will not only bring them alive for you, but will help you to hear the music, the pace and the rhythm of the language.

It will help you to evoke the pictures. It will also help your writing to be more beguiling. As a playwright you should attempt to be a reasonably good amateur actor. Reading aloud is also the only way to time a play and a stopwatch should be one of your first investments. Why not act out the previous passage - complete with sound effects?

Tapping the Listener's Imagination

When you are writing a radio play, remember two things:

1. That you are writing for **a single listener**. That single listener may hopefully be multiplied by hundreds of thousands, but you should write the play as if it takes place in the privacy of a single person's imagination.

2. Try to think of what can **only** happen in radio. In that way you will explore the medium at its most imaginative.

Although the structure of radio plays and of novels are quite different, they can act on the imagination in a similar manner. George Eliot said of the novel: 'No species of art is so free from rigid requirements. Like crystalline masses it may take any form, and yet be beautiful; we have only to pour in the right elements - observation, humour and passion'. Henry James wrote: 'The novelist competes with his brother the painter in his attempt to render the look of things, that conveys their meanings, to catch the relief, the colour, the expression, the surface, the substance of the human spectacle.' I believe these thoughts apply even more to the creation of a radio play: a mysterious process, which is one of implicit connivance between playwright and listener.

Of course the director, the actors and the technicians also have a hand. It is partly this teamwork that makes the creation of a radio play such a joy; a joy that can come as a reward in the normally solitary life of the playwright. Radio is very much a writer's medium.

Donald McWhinnie, in *The Art of Radio*, observes: 'The world of visual detail which the listener creates is a world of limitless dimension; the images may be vivid, but they have no specific proportions; they exist in a world that is largely a dream world. The radio performance works on the mind in the same way as poetry does; it liberates and evokes.'

Beginning with an Image

In a radio play, language - sometimes assisted by sound effects, variety of acoustic spaces, music and comparative silence - has to accomplish far more than in any other medium. The language has to tell the story, reveal character and draw pictures in the theatre of the listener's mind.

Perhaps it is not surprising that many radio plays are first triggered by an image. For example the playwright, Michael Campbell, saw a man with his shoes and trousers on, standing up to his knees in the sea, playing a violin. Michael was shy. He never asked the man why he was doing this. Instead he used the image to start on a creative journey and arrived at his own explanation in his play, *The Man Who Stood In The Sea*.

Another playwright, Juliet Ace, was fascinated by the story of Coco, the parrot, whose cage sat on the bar of the Hotel Commodore, where journalists used to congregate in Beirut. Her play takes place in 1982 immediately before the Israeli invasion of Lebanon. Coco had been taught by hard-bitten reporters to swear in twenty-two different languages. Walid the barman was so jealous of the attention that the clients paid to Coco, that under cover of an Israeli bombardment, he shot the parrot. *Lobby Talk* was a 'pure' radio play, an aural experience that explored and extended the medium and that could not be expressed in any other form. The parrot is the narrator - until he is shot.

In performance this excerpt from the beginning of the play lasted exactly three minutes. Again I suggest that you should try performing - and timing it - yourself. Be a parrot!

> (THE GENERAL BACKGROUND NOISE IN THE
> HOTEL FOYER IS MUFFLED. WE ARE IN THE
> PARROT'S CAGE, WHICH IS COVERED BY A
> CLOTH.)

ANNOUNCER: 'Lobby Talk', a play dedicated to Coco the parrot by Juliet Ace and Vic Aicken, with Steve Hodson as Coco and Andrew Sachs as Walid.

COCO: When anyone asks why I am covered with a cloth at this time of day, Walid tells them I am getting on, and need an afternoon nap. The truth is, that whilst I could give him a good few years, my stamina, wit and untiring ability to communicate and delight, outstrip his meagre efforts. However, when he thinks to punish me, he does me a favour. Teatime at the Commodore is dead time. The faded Brits teeter in on high heels, bleating for toasted teacakes, but settling for sticky pastry drenched in honey. (SQUAWKS) But I am being remiss. My name is Coco. I might have preferred the dignity of Charles or Winston or Dwight . . . but in these difficult times, Coco is probably safer.   My owner, a journalist whose name does not spring immediately to mind, left me here some years ago. Fouad, the Manager, could see that the ladies and gentlemen of the press, far from home and family, would appreciate someone who could speak to them in their own language and be sympathetic in their darker moments. So here I am.
(SQUAWKS TWICE) I rank pretty high in parrot terms. I may not match particular parrots who appear in novels of magical realism…. But - and this is important - I exist. I am internationally famous and I have learnt to speak more languages than any other parrot I have heard of. You must understand however that I cannot separate one language from another. . I do not have that facility. Therefore I hear all languages as one. A language whose vocabulary extends into millions of words. More complex than Esperanto and without accent. What I hear, you will hear.

(THE CLOTH IS WHIPPED OFF THE CAGE. THE HOTEL SOUNDS ARE AUGMENTED TO PROPER PITCH)

WALID: OK. Wake up. But behave yourself. One word out of place, I might shut you up for good.

COCO: (INTERNAL VOICE) Boring little man. (ALOUD. SQUAWKS) Gimme a scotch.

WALID: Shut up.

COCO: Gimme a scotch. A large one you fool.
WALID: (HIGH PITCHED) Shut up! Shut up!

(COCO WHISTLES THE FIRST COUPLE OF BARS OF THE MARSEILLAISE HITTING A FINAL WRONG NOTE)

WALID: (OFF) One day he'll open his mouth once too often.

COCO: (INTERNAL VOICE) And so will he.

The author elegantly solves the problem of the characters' speaking many different languages. Also you will notice how she builds up and gradually pieces together both the narrative and the pictures. In radio the unfolding of the story and the encourage-ment of the listeners to create pictures in their minds are crucially connected.

Considering Shakespeare And Other Audio Playwrights

Shakespeare, writing 300 years before the invention of the medium, was, paradoxically, an excellent radio playwright. His language is full of pictures: of descriptions of scenery, of dress and of characters. The audience (from the Latin *audire:* to hear) used to go to the Globe Theatre not to 'see', but to 'hear' a play. There was virtually no scenery, just costume and a few props.   The groundlings and the gallery were encouraged to create the scenery in their heads.

In the 20th Century there were hardly any major playwrights who did not learn, develop and/or master their art in radio before moving on to theatre, film and TV.   Samuel Beckett, Robert Bolt, Caryl Churchill, Ethan Coen, Anthony Minghella, Arthur Miller, John Mortimer, Clifford Odets, Harold Pinter, Tom Stoppard, Dylan Thomas, Sue Townsend and Fay Weldon are just a few names that spring to mind; and most of them have frequently revisited radio, their first love.

In radio they learnt how the spoken word, almost alone, can with skill and economy accomplish everything.   It is in radio that they have come nearer to fulfilling three of my favourite precepts: 'Industry, intelligence and imagination' (Gwen Ffrancon Davies), 'True, clear and interesting' (Prunella Scales) and 'Faith, hope and clarity' (Dorothy Reynolds)

Understanding What Makes A Good Radio Play

A little history

In radio you can have a cast of thousands and you can span centuries and continents.   You can make the equivalent of a film like *The Lord of the Rings* for a thousandth of the cost.   You can also enter the recesses of a person's mind.   It can be the most intimate of media.   It is a wonderfully liberating medium, yet the craft of writing a radio play is one of the hardest to master.

But what essentially makes a *good* radio play?   In order to gain an insight into this, I am going to give you a little history.   Most of the early radio plays in the 1920's were adaptations of stage plays.   As Cecil Lewis said in 1923:

"So far, we have largely contented ourselves (I think wisely) with Shakespeare, whose amazing beauty lies almost entirely in the spoken word as a means of presenting character and situation.   No better plays for broadcasting could have been written."

One of the first plays written specifically for Radio was *Danger* by the novelist, Richard Hughes.   He wrote it in 1923 in twenty-four hours to fill a gap in the schedules.   In an article in the Radio Times he advised:

> "The scene of the play is laid in a mine, and to help the atmosphere, it is suggested that listeners might well sit in darkness to correspond with the play's setting."

The play began with the speech: 'The lights have gone out'.   It could only work on radio. The listener was invited to identify with a group of trapped miners. Radio was beginning already to come to terms with a mass, as opposed to a West End, audience. There was one exception: the article advised parents not to allow their children to listen, lest they be frightened. Audience response was enthusiastic. Over a thousand letters and postcards arrived at the BBC, including one from the leading actress Ellen Terry:

> "No greater performance have I ever heard, which has produced such a thrill on an unseen audience, another step forward has been taken by the BBC."

Shortly afterwards, the blind writer R.C Scriven wrote a play about an eye operation called *The Single Taper*. From the start writers were thinking, 'What makes a radio play different from other plays ?'

The history of Radio Drama and, for a brief period when it nearly became a major art form, the history of Television Drama can be enlightening to the aspiring radio writer.

Major Art Forms

In television forty years ago four or five new plays by new or major playwrights were broadcast every week.   In 1965 *Cathy Come Home* by Jeremy Sandford and *A Breach in the Wall*, a new play about a miracle at Canterbury by Ray Lawler, attracted audiences of twelve million and that was when only about half the population of the United Kingdom had access to television. In the North of England, men were leaving the pubs at ten past nine (in those days the news lasted only fifteen minutes) to be home for

BBC1's *The Wednesday Play*. It is revealing to compare these figures to the audience, pro rata, for *Eastenders*. It might have been better both artistically and commercially, if television had remained writer, rather than management led. In the 1990's under John Birt's stewardship radio showed signs of aping television's mistakes, but fortunately both staff morale and the quality and quantity of radio drama output appear to be recovering.

In his preface to a collection of Best Radio Plays for 1988, Richard Imison wrote:

> "Taken on their own the statistics of radio drama as an active part of British cultural life between 1978 and 1988 are really rather impressive...' There were 'some three and a half thousand original radio plays broadcast by the BBC. These plays had been commissioned for the most part from among the hundred thousand completed scripts and synopses submitted to the Radio Drama department during this period. More than five thousand writers were regularly involved in writing radio plays and many more occasionally gave the medium a try. All these figures are dwarfed however by the number of times individual listeners switched on a radio play in the course of the past ten years: a prodigious ten billion."

Radio Drama has a magnificent past and hopefully a bright future in the form perhaps not of radio, but of 'sound' or 'audio' drama on CD, the Internet and other means of dissemination.

Meanwhile with its new digital channel BBC7 as well as with Radios 3 and 4, all of which are streamed on www.bbc.co.uk, the BBC is maintaining its role as a guardian of the great British cultural tradition of Radio Drama.

It is as a lover of the medium from my first childhood memories and as a script editor and producer of some thirty years experience that I am writing this book. I invite you to share the firm and fervent hope that audio drama is an art form that still has far to go.

You have no doubt bought this book because you are interested in writing and selling a radio play, feature or short story. Now let us get down to practicalities.

2 Starting a Radio Play

Getting Started

Establishing a routine and ritual

As a writer you will have to acquire discipline.   You may need to learn to impose regular hours and rituals upon yourself.   You should try and discover the right pattern: one you will stick to and which yields the best results.

Fay Weldon, one of the busiest and more productive writers, that I know, says that the only time to write is early in the morning; but that one must sharpen one's pencils and have one's paper ready or prepare one's computer the night before. In that way one will have as few distractions as possible and hopefully the muse will not depart, before one gets down to work.   She goes on to say that the same rules apply as used to apply to writing a school essay. Some people will prepare very well. Others will do it in a desperate last minute rush. She could not resist adding: 'Often the harder you try, the worse marks you will get.'

The late Peter Tinniswood, author of many stylish and highly original radio plays, used to get up every day at about 6.30 a.m. and be at his computer by 8. He then worked till 11.30 when he went shopping and paid a short visit to a pub - in the summer to see a bit of the test match. After a light lunch he would work until about 4.30 p.m. when he would pay a second brief visit to the pub, often with a mate like myself. Thus on his writing days he worked concentratedly for about six hours.

Mike Walker, author of hundreds of radio plays and creative features, finds starting a new project the hardest challenge. So he gears himself in, only spends 10 minutes on the first day and then maybe half an hour on the second. On the third day he gets down to his regular routine of starting when his wife leaves to teach at 8.30 in the morning and he works through to lunch. He often takes an oxygen inducing, weight reducing cycle ride in the early afternoon. Incidentally he once said: "Drama is like a bicycle - if it ain't going somewhere, you fall over". He then works through again from 4.30 - 6.30. If he has a deadline he will work straight through to bedtime without a break.

Tina Pepler, one of the most original playwrights in the country, spends a long preparation period, in which she makes hundreds of notes on cards.   She then creates or discovers the shape of her play from her arrangement of the cards; like completing a jigsaw puzzle. The actual writing of the play comes last and is a very fast and concentrated process.

Colin Haydn Evans, author of radio plays on a remarkable diversity of subjects and in an equally remarkable diversity of styles, is highly disciplined; though as he says himself, 'perhaps not in a formal way'.   When he has a play commissioned he calculates precisely how long it will take him to write, on the assumption that he will complete three minutes of play a day. (His first draft is composed entirely of dialogue, with no directions or effects.)   Thus a sixty-minute play will take twenty working days. Since, he says this target is well under his usual, average output he can be confident that he will always meet the deadline.

Peter Terson will sit in cafés sketching people and out of these characters and situations his plays will grow and evolve. His play scripts are wonderfully picturesque.   At one time he wrote and illustrated them on wallpaper.   We used to have to crawl around the office floor to read them and to enjoy the pictures. How to get a producer down on his knees!

I do not believe Hilaire Belloc wrote any plays, but when asked why he kept on writing, at least one hundred and forty books, he replied, 'To keep my children in jewellery and caviar'. Nick McCarty simply puts the notice 'Mortgage!' in front of him on the desk.

Each writer, by trial and error must find their own method. If you work to a disciplined pattern a great deal of creativity will happen during your 'fallow' periods. I have been lucky enough to write this book mostly during short breaks between other projects, beside the sea in Vietnam and Cambodia. I find that most of my memories and ideas come to me, after several hours at my laptop, when eating alone or swimming; or when in England, when walking or gardening. Also one will quite often wake up at night with a new idea or the solution to a problem. Be sure to have a notebook and pen handy to jot it down. As a Jewish writer friend of mine says, 'Miracles are damned carefully prepared!'

Grabbing the Audience

The beginning of the play

BBC Radio 4's commissioning brief for the 45 minute Afternoon Play slot, states that programmes should have 'clear and beguiling openings and use their opening credits to set up the play and make listening as easy as possible'.

In radio you do not have a *captive* audience, who has paid for a seat, who might be embarrassed to leave and who will therefore give the play a chance to develop. On TV and more so on radio the audience can very quickly switch off; first mentally and then physically. As Sidney Newman, the charismatic and vulgar Head of BBC TV Drama in the sixties, said: 'Catch them by the goolies as they get up to switch the set off and you've got them for half an hour.' Radio is a less sensational, but potentially a more beguiling medium than television. Having made the unusual career move from TV to Radio, I think I am entitled to make this claim!.

The switch off button is never far off. As a writer you probably have about a minute, two at the outside, to engage your listener. However wonderful the rest of the play, if your beginning does not captivate the listeners, they will never stay to be enchanted.

Examples of beginnings

Let's look at the beginning of a famous radio play, first broadcast in 1957:

ANNOUNCER: This is the BBC Third Programme. We present a play by Giles Cooper entitled, 'The Disagreeable Oyster'.

BUNDY: You can say that again.

ANNOUNCER: 'The Disagreeable Oyster.'

BUNDY: They do disagree with me, but how was I to know when I stood on the steps of the

Rosedene Family and Commercial Hotel,
thinking that the world was my oyster that –

BUNDY MINOR: Begin at the beginning.

BUNDY: And the beginning is at twelve o'clock on a
                   Saturday morning in my office at Craddock's
                   Calculators Ltd.

It is a period piece, but no less entertaining for that. It is about a
very ordinary person in a very ordinary situation and yet because
the story is presented in a stylish and amusing way, one wants to
listen on. This beginning conveys necessary information without
spelling it out in an obvious, boring or clumsy way. It also begins
to establish the conventions, that Bundy, the central character, can
step outside the action of the play and talk to the announcer, and
that Bundy is divided into two parts, the more thoughtful being
Bundy Minor.

  Let's look at the beginning of a more recent play, and see
how much information the playwright divulges in an oblique and
entertaining manner.

                   (MUSIC: OLD RECORDING OF THE SONG 'LOVE
                   IS THE SWEETEST THING ')

ANNOUNCER: 'Hard of Hearing' by Colin Haydn Evans

                   (FADE MUSIC. SFX OF TWO PEOPLE EATING
                   BREAKFAST).

JUNE: I was reading the other day of this man who
                   used to talk to hedgehogs. The only problem he
                   said was that he never knew the meaning of
                   what he said to them.

                   (BRIAN SIGHS)

JUNE: Lyme Regis. I think he lived in Lyme Regis.

BRIAN: Er-hum.

JUNE: He did not know the meaning of what he said
           to them.

(PAUSE)

BRIAN: June, are you trying to say something?

JUNE: Yes.

BRIAN: Over breakfast?

JUNE: It's Saturday, Brian.

BRIAN: Ruddy Mecca, if you ask me. Light at the end
           of the week's tunnel.

JUNE: Didn't Maureen used to have a residential
           caravan near there? It's in Dorset isn't it, Lyme
           Regis? They used to spend the second half of
           September in it.

(BRIAN SIGHS AGAIN)

JUNE: He went on to say that the principle could be
           equally well applied to the Colorado Beetle.
           Talking to them, I mean. He felt it might be
           good news for potato farmers.

BRIAN: Toast.

JUNE: (TO HERSELF) He said grazing her eyes with
           his.

BRIAN: If you want any more there won't be enough.

FX: SHE PUTS ANOTHER SLICE INTO
           TOASTER

JUNE: (ALOUD) I like people who do silly things. I think it's comforting.

(TO HERSELF) If you don't say something soon you page three moron you're going to get this piece of cremated bread right up your pre-soaked shirt. Fancy that do you?

(ALOUD) What Love?

This is the beginning of a marvellous comedy, in which Brian spends Saturday morning attempting to mend the washing machine and spends half the play with his head stuck in it - an interesting acoustic. (He has programmed the door to remain open while the drum revolves and his tie gets caught round it). Not unlike *The Disagreeable Oyster*., the play starts in an everyday, conventional setting with ordinary people, though, hopefully, the listener senses that an intriguing story is about to unfold. It also establishes one character's inner voice; that the other character cannot hear.

In talking to aspiring radio playwrights, who ask me what I am looking for, I often say: 'Please, surprise me. Please give me something I have never encountered before.' But I also say, 'If you can start a play with ordinary people in an ordinary setting, with whom many listeners will identify; then if you can make that really entertaining and different; I shall be delighted.'

Let's look at the beginning of play that could hardly be more different. *Babylon Has Fallen* by John Fletcher, has a much a less conventional setting - that of a Victorian tropical island where Augustus Hare, an old Etonian roué with a Malaysian harem and David Worth, a non-conformist evangelist with a band of pious disciples, confront one another. John Fletcher, who is something of a visionary, has allowed his imagination free rein. He also wrote a stage version of the play, in which, at the beginning, the characters were brought on and introduced to the audience. This is he felt would not be so compelling in the radio version, which starts as follows:

(HIGHLY DRAMATIC, VICTORIAN ORGAN MUSIC)

DAVID: One Morning the Lord God Ravished I. As I did sit at Sunday service, the sun full in the aisle, playing a voluntary upon the organ, a flare of raw light did hit my body, burnt so strong, I could see every bone glowing within my hands. While all about I the world fell dark and dead. And as He did ravish I, the Lord God implanted within I the seed of wisdom. 'Go, David Worth,' He said, 'leave your Babylonian captivity here in Bristol. Seek out a place unsullied by human habitation and there build for me the Temple of the new Jerusalem'.

(FADE ORGAN MUSIC)

From that moment there has been no distraction in my life. At night I studied the holy texts of Revelation, seeking to understand the sacred principles of Divine Geometry. Upon old ocean charts I found an island, the Keeling Coco Island, lying deep in the wastes of the Great Southern Ocean. Myself, all my companions, my wife and children, my faithful servant Elisha all scrimped and saved, husbanded our scarce resources, until one day last Spring after many hardships, us set sail from our native Bristol, down the Gorge of Avon and out upon the broad ocean, committing ourselves to the perilous deep.

(BRING UP AND SWELL SAILING SHIP CUTTING THROUGH HEAVY SEAS AND INTO THE NEXT SCENE)

Here we have a larger than life character in a relatively unusual situation. However what this beginning has in common with the two earlier examples is that it is starting to tell a story. If these beginnings have done their job properly for you, as they have for me, I am intrigued, even compelled, to listen on, to know what is going to happen next. Incidentally the fading of the organ music subtly directs the listener away from the chapel and inside David's head, rather as one might track into a close-up on film..

Knowing Where To Start Your Play

The beginning is vital.   As a script editor and drama director for over thirty years, I must have commented upon tens of thousands of scripts. One of the questions I most frequently ask promising writers is, 'Do you think you have begun your play in the right place?' This is because I have got into the habit of making a note, of *where* I first became involved and really wanted to know, what was going to happen next.

Page 27 in a sixty-page script sticks in my mind.   This perhaps, on average, is the point, when I say to myself, particularly where a promising new writer is concerned: 'Ah, this is interesting, at last. This is what the play is about. This is where the story really begins. This is *why* you are writing the play'.   Very often up to this point you, the aspiring writer, may have been writing yourself into the play; discovering what it is about.   You have gone through the necessary process of producing a first draft. But I must warn you, that very probably the script is not yet ready to submit to a busy script editor or producer, who might well reject it out of hand.

I did not work with David Zane Mairowitz on his play *Dictator Gal* and do not know whether this was his original opening. But it is certainly gripping:

> (FEEBLE BREATHING OF PATIENT. ELECTRO-CARDIOGRAM CONNECTED TO ELECTRONIC STETHOSCOPE. HEARTBEAT AUDIBLE: SLOW, IRREGULAR.. REGULAR HUM OF HOSPITAL MACHINERY ESTABLISHES.

DOOR QUIETLY CLOSED. QUIET FOOTSTEPS.
DOCTOR HUMS 'STRANGER IN PARADISE'.
CURTAIN FOLDED BACK. PATIENT BREATHING.)

DOCTOR: (Murmuring to himself: writing on chart)
            Pressure. 40 over 10; pulse - 30 - 30? Not worth
            it. Bon Voyage Mr - Mr - er - Flannigan.-

            (PLUG PULLED. MACHINERY COMES TO A
            NOISY DEFINITIVE STOP. GURGLING NOISE
            FROM PATIENT. BECOMES LOUDER. BODY
            MOVEMENT UNDE SHEETS. GASPING.
            LONG DEATH THROES.)

            (Naturally) Shh! You'll wake the other patients.

            (DOCTOR LEAVES ROOM STILL HUMMING
            'STRANGER IN PARADISE'. THE PATIENT GIVES A
            FINAL GASP. CONTINUOUS BLEEP OF LIFE
            SUPPORT SYSTEM INDICATES THAT PATIENT'S
            HEART HAS STOPPED)

Would you want to listen on?

Writing For A Sophisticated Audience

Tina Pepler's *Easy Traumas* was written for a sophisticated Radio 3 audience, who are probably prepared to devote more concentration to listening, than a Radio 4, Afternoon Play audience, who may be distracted by housework, driving or small children.   It is not so much that the people who listen to drama on Radios 2, 3 and 4 are different. In fact audience research indicates, that they are probably the same people, but that they are listening in different circumstances.

Easy Traumas concerns an angelic agency that helps you to cope with the worst crises in your life: death, divorce, house-moving, loss of a banana milk-shake, etc; though the listener will only learn this as the play develops.

ANNOUNCER: Introducing the Easy Traumas Agency.
              Take it away Castor Sugar.

C. SUGAR: Hi!

ANNOUNCER: And Pollux.

POLLUX: Hello there.

(SNAFFLE DRUM)

ANNOUNCER: Deborah Makepeace plays Castor Sugar,
              Steve Hodson plays Pollux, Christian
              Rodska plays Barny and Liz Goulding plays
              Wilma in Easy Traumas by Tina Pepler.

POLLUX: Let go into the healing power of hatred.

C. SUGAR: Get smart about falling apart.

POLLUX: Get wise to your own demise.

C. SUGAR: We work fast from the outside in. No
              introspection.

POLLUX: Don't think.

C. SUGAR: Don't wonder about what went wrong.

POLLUX: Whatever you do don't think.

C. SUGAR: Just do it.

POLLUX: Your thoughts will catch up with your
              instincts.

C. SUGAR: Easy Traumas.

POLLUX:	Bizarre, yes. Cruel, perhaps. Indifferent, almost certainly. But we know what we are saying.
C. SUGAR:	Are we shallow?
POLLUX:	Are we cruel?
C. SUGAR:	You bet your bottom we are.
POLLUX:	But we're very good communicators.
C. SUGAR:	You need us.
POLLUX:	Barnie.
C. SUGAR:	You may not know it, but you need us.

(START TO FADE DRUM AND SPEECH)

POLLUX:	Let go.
C. SUGAR:	Let go.
POLLUX:	Let go.

As Giles Cooper in *The Disagreeable Oyster*, Tina Pepler has the announcer enter the play to interact with the characters.

Fay Weldon has commented wryly and wittily on most aspects of contemporary life, so why not on the writing and producing of a radio play? Here is the beginning of *The Hole in the Top of the World*, a BBC/Los Angeles Theatre Works co-production, starring Walter Matthau. Fay Weldon imagines that Matt is making a radio play about his life story:

(THE SOUND OF WHISTLING ANTARCTIC
WINDS. IT DIES AS MATT SPEAKS. MATT IS
60'ISH, EDUCATED, CHARMING, DANGEROUS,

TRANSATLANTIC. HE'S BEEN EVERYWHERE,
DONE EVERYTHING.)

MATT: Did you get that, radio freaks? That wasn't the
               desert winds over the High Sierra. That was the
               winds whistling in Antarctica. What you're
               hearing is the icy bit at the bottom of the world.
               Though, as they tell you in Australia, since
               there's no up and down in space, it's as
               reasonable to call it the top as the bottom.
               That way the Australians can get to be not
               down under but on top. If that suits them,
               that's okay by me. I'm not in the business of
               making anyone feel bad. All I ever wanted to
               do was move the world on a bit; understand the
               material universe. Why are scientists so
               unpopular? Is there something wrong with
               harnessing the power of the sun, curing
               melanoma? You people out there are
               ungrateful. I won't say stupid - you'd switch
               off. And then I'd have wasted good money on
               this sound studio, hiring these airwaves.

               I know I called you freaks, but don't take it too
               hard: face it you're listening to the radio, not
               watching TV, and that makes you the last of the
               listeners; all you want is someone's voice to fill
               the space between your ears. What you want is
               what God never gave us. A story with a
               beginning a middle, and an end; a point and a
               purpose. Some kind of pattern in amongst the
               chaos. All I ever wanted , or worked for. Now
               they're all at it. Catastrophe Theory, Fractals.
               My generation paved the way: and is anyone
               grateful? No. Listen again.

(SX. WIND. ADD SEAGULLS)

That fooled you. Seagulls signify a coast.
A coastline in Antarctica? Well okay.

(ADD HOOTING OWLS)

Okay, make that night. The coast of
Antarctica at night.

(ADD TRAFFIC SOUNDS)

A little town at night on the coast of
Antarctica.

(ADD POLICE SIRENS)

A big town at night on some cliff on
Antarctica.

(FADE POLICE SIRENS. ADD TOLLING OF
CHURCH BELLS)

A churchyard? No - here the mind boggles.
That's what I had in mind for you, the boggling
of the mind. Overload. Even if I told you that
was a high wind in Jamaica

(LOSE CHURCH BELLS. INTRODUCE WIND PLUS
THE BANANA BOAT SONG)

you'd still have trouble. So forget it. Let's have
some silence.

(SILENCE. HOLD IT)

Silence is frightening. Nothingness.

Silence is certainly powerful. Donald McWhinnie in 1959 in *The Art of Radio* quotes a woman, a devotee of the 'telly', who referred to the radio as the 'silent'.

McWhinnie wrote that she had stumbled on a truth: 'paradoxically there is silence at the heart of the radio experience, it might almost be unspoken communication between writer and listener'.   Also silence is the frame within which a radio play takes place.

Setting The Scene And The Atmosphere

I am going to end this chapter with an excerpt from one of the most enchanting plays, it has been my privilege to direct. Unlike the other examples it is a not from an original play. It is a dramatisation of a Russian novel. Dramatisation is not easy and I would never encourage an aspiring writer to attempt to adapt a novel and still less a TV or screenplay, until they have had at least two or three original plays produced for radio.

> <u>(THE SEVENTH SYMPHONY OF THEODORAKIS</u>
> <u>ESTABLISHES ITSELF THEN PLAYS VERY GENTLY</u>
> <u>BEHIND THE FOLLOWING)</u>

LEONID: It is twenty-five years since I gave my word to the old lady, Sarma. What happened, happened in the time of my childhood. It has probably happened to lots of children, who are perhaps afraid of not being believed. So they kept silent.

> <u>(MUSIC FADES)</u>

They at least will believe me.

> <u>(THE MUSIC GENTLY RE-EMERGES)</u>

At this point I must issue a warning. I would not waste your time on some harmless, if amusing little fairy tale. You may find it difficult, but I beg you to try to break through the barrier of disbelief.

I have learnt, you see, that the truth, which exists within us, is immensely greater than the truth, which is revealed to us in the form of rules and laws in this world of ours.

(WE STAY WITH THE MUSIC FOR A MOMENT AND THEN, GENTLY AT FIRST, THE SOUND OF A DISTANT STEAM TRAIN EMERGES FROM WITHIN IT).

A miracle is something that occurs in spite of and contrary to everything. According to the rules it does not happen. Consequently when a miracle does take place, it does so in defiance of the rules. You've never experienced a miracle? Not even a trifling, little miracle? I can help. Listen. No need to go to the ends of the earth. All you need is to go to the town of Irkutsk, board the Irkutsk to Slyudyanka train and sit on the left hand side of the carriage, facing forward.

(TRAIN WHISTLES. MAINTAIN STEAM TRAIN AND MUSIC IN BACKGROUND)

ANNOUNCER: 'The Year of Miracle and Grief' by Leonid Borodin, dramatised by Nick McCarty. Leonid Borodin was born in 1938 on the shores of Lake Baikal. Since 1966 he has been imprisoned twice for his Orthodox Christian beliefs. He was finally released in 1987. We present Steve Hodson as Leonid in 'The Year of Miracle and Grief'

(WE MIX TO INTERIOR OF TRAIN CARRIAGE)

YOUNG LEO: Will it be much longer, Papa?

FATHER: Not much longer, Leonid. Go to sleep boy.

And so, the scene and the atmosphere are set and now the play proper can begin.   Here the writer has promised to take us on a journey into and out of childhood, to tell us a story, to share a vision and to reveal a mystery.   You can hardly do better than that.

You will note that the directions in this excerpt identify the music. In fact Nick McCarty talked to me (the director) about how important the music would be in establishing and sustaining an atmosphere of power and mystery.   He suggested the Greek composer Theodorakis. Then he and I did a lot of listening, while acting out and timing some of the narrative passages, and seeing how we could engineer music and language to blend effectively together.

I should always encourage the writer to do this as much as possible at an early stage. The writer is responsible not just for the language, but for the entire sound track: sound effects, music, acoustic and silence as well.   As director I want to know everything that the writer hears in his head.   I want all these elements to be in the script as part of the overall composition, just as I would want all the instrumental parts to be there, if I were a conducting an orchestra.

You will note that several of the examples of beginnings of plays, that I have given consist of a single voice narrative, mostly by a central character talking in the first person. A few years ago the narrator rather went out of fashion, but now appears to be coming back. The power and beauty of the single human voice, well produced and acted, can provide a compelling and cajoling way into a play. If kept fairly short, the contrast of 'opening up' from this overture into a scene in a concrete place, with more than one voice, can both fulfil a promise and be quite arresting. It can be the second movement of your symphony.

We shall say more about how to continue a play in the next chapter.

3 Structuring a Radio Play

Starting At The End

In the last chapter we looked at how to begin a play. In order to arrive at an overall structure or design, at a shape that will continuously captivate the listener, it would not be a bad idea at this stage to think about the ending.

'In my beginning is my end' (T.S. Eliot's *Four Quartets*), contains an important truth for dramatists. Perhaps, more appositely, this should be reversed: 'In my end is my beginning.' Some dramatists may have to complete the first draft to discover where they should start from. They may end up like the Irishman, who when asked how to get to Castlebar, replied, 'If I wanted to get to Castlebar, I wouldn't start from here in the first place'.

Some writers have no idea at all, when they start, either what they want to say or where the characters are leading them. The process of writing itself will be a journey of discovery.

Peter Tinniswood used to say that if he knew the end of the play when he was a quarter of the way in, he knew it was going to work. If he didn't, he might still solve the ending by going back to the beginning and writing that in a different way.

We looked at the beginning of Colin Haydn Evans' play *Hard of Hearing* in the last chapter and will look at the ending of it later in this chapter. He rarely knows how a play is going to end, when he starts it. For him the ending is in a state of constant flux and can change several times.   Knowing the conclusion beforehand, would be like the tail wagging the dog. He would always feel that he had to move down a certain road in a precise way to arrive at a set destination.

He goes on to say that the characters themselves dictate most of what will take place. Some will flatly refuse certain endings - others demand them. If he tries to impose a false conclusion (false that is in terms of the *real* theme) they revolt by withholding meaningful dialogue, resorting solely to cliché. He can literally then no longer 'write' them. Only when he lets them have their heads again will they resume speaking to him.

Thus, Haydn Evans claims, when writers claim that characters come 'alive' it is no exaggeration. Writing he says is not the lonely business it is popularly thought to be. Everyday the writer walks into a room full of people and yesterday's silent, often intriguing conversations reopen. He says 'I am not sure this is entirely healthy - but happen it does! There are lines in my plays that I quite genuinely feel have nothing at all to do with me. It was the characters solely. All I did was listen.'

Other writers will have a clear purpose and a definite ending in mind from the start. There are no absolutes about this. In fact one of the joys of working on and listening to really good radio plays is to appreciate how different is the approach of each writer.

In any case I have put this chapter next, because I think it a good idea to be wrestling with the problem of structure at an early stage in the process of writing a play. If the first draft has a structure which is attractive to the listener, then one may be on one's way to writing a hugely popular play.

If you have a beginning and an end in mind, it may be easier to plan the richness and variety of the journey in between. On the other hand you may lose something of the spontaneity of discovery. I am reminded of Jean Luc Godard, the French film director, who when asked whether he thought his plays should have a beginning, a middle and an end, replied in his charming French accent, 'Yes definitely, but not necessarily in that order.'

Giving Shape

Try applying your mind to the end of the play as you might to the end of a pilgrimage, to give shape and meaning to your journey, to your narrative. It does not matter if the end changes radically in the course of writing the play. This will probably be because you have found ways of improving it. However it can be a good idea to start with a shape to give yourself an even better shape.

Why not ask yourself, 'Why am I writing this play?' 'What do I want to say?' , 'What thoughts and feelings do I want to leave the listener with at the end of the play?' It may be helpful to examine the endings of two of the plays, whose beginnings we examined in the last chapter. First *The Year of Miracle and Grief.*

The novel, of course, already has an ending. Thus, although the beginning and the ending of the dramatisation may not be exactly the same as in the novel, you will have a good idea as to where you are aiming. A note of explanation: Ri has been young Leonid's first love.

LEONID: We were to move again to another school in Siberia. I wanted to say good bye to Ri at the end of the term

(GENTLE STEAMING OF STATIONARY TRAIN)

RI: I have to go Leon

YOUNG LEO: Yes. I - I will always remember you Rienka.

(FOOTSTEPS AND DISTANT ECHOING HOOT OF ENGINE)

LEONID: She climbed up the step into the carriage and I never again saw the girl from Dead Man's Crag

(TRAIN GENTLY DEPARTS. FADE TO SILENCE)

YOUNG LEO: Vayerka gave me his three bladed pen-knife and Svetka gave me a book and I said good-bye to them.

LEONID: And good-bye to Lake Baikal. I remembered Ri holding a yellow snow-drop in her hand on the first day of the thaw

(GENTLE STEAMING AGAIN)

And then we too got into the train and that parting was without real pain. A childhood remains a childhood

(THE STEAM TRAIN STARTS TO DEPART)

My memories of what had happened on the shores of Lake Baikal gradually blurred and, only if I find myself alone on a moonlit night, will the crescent of the new moon cause me to return to the sadness of the past.   Possibly all my past has been nothing more than a preparation for my return.

(THE TRAIN BEGINS TO SPEED UP. DISTANT HOOT)

I feel sure that one day I shall go to Irkutsk,

(THE THEME MUSIC FROM THEODOKARIS STARTS VERY GENTLY)

board a train to Slyudyanka, and sit on the left hand side of the carriage. Then when the break in the mountains unveils the blue water and the brown crags, I shall discover for myself the essence of what is called the meaning of life. A miracle? Oh Yes!

(SWELL MUSIC AND TRAIN AND THEN INTO CLOSING CREDITS)

If you refer back to the beginning, you will see the connection with the end and perhaps, without reading the novel or listening to the play, you could have a go at writing the journey in between.   You will probably not sell the result, but it could be an interesting, learning exercise.

Now that we know something of the process by which he arrived there, let us have a look at the ending of the Colin Haydn Evans' *Hard of Hearing*.

It was a half hour play and for almost half of it Brian's head is stuck in the washing machine with his tie caught in the works. He goes on and on criticising June, until eventually she flips and turns on the machine. There's a stifled squawk and a horrible grinding noise and in the next scene Brian wakes up in hospital having suffered concussion and a broken nose. At this point we begin to hear his inner thoughts for the first time. Perhaps, unlike his wife, he has up to now, for many years, suppressed his thoughts. The play ends with a kind of reconciliation and with June and Brian going to bed together at three o'clock in the afternoon:

BRIAN: (<u>TO HIMSELF</u>) Being angry is being recognised. June got the brunt of it, I suppose. Kept asking, 'Why!?' Never saw that if I knew why, I'd never have been like that in the first place.

JUNE: (<u>ALOUD, ON ECHO FROM PAST</u>) How do you mean: 'thinking of me'?

BRIAN: (<u>TO HIMSELF</u>) That's how the fondness goes , I suppose. Nobody keeping their lives to themselves. Trying to make others do their living for them. Turning marriage into an encounter group and sex into a bloody space launch. (<u>PAUSE</u>) The snag is, I think, when you get it right, you never really know. That leaves the door open for someone to tell you it isn't. That way you end up with your head in a washing machine. Brainwashing!

JUNE: (<u>TO HERSELF</u>) And why will I stay? They say people grow lonely as they get older. Then they need to turn to someone. Forty four's not that old really. You never know, he may turn out quite nicely in the end.

BRIAN: (<u>TO HIMSELF</u>) I never wanted to be understood. Just liked.

JUNE: (<u>TO HERSELF</u>) Marriage isn't a miracle after all. It's just two people looking for one, which makes it twice as hard to find.

(SHE STIRS IN BED AND SIGHS)

JUNE: (ALOUD) There's still time before tea, Brian.

BRIAN: What? Oh yeah.

(MUSIC: 'LOVE IS THE SWEETEST THING')

The shape of the play and the comedy give the author the opportunity to share with us in some depth his thoughts on the nature of marriage. Notice that in a sense the ending of this play is contained in, or at least promised by, the beginning.

Planning The Structure In Between

So how do you get from the beginning to the end? Here are a few pointers.

1. Make sure that your listener always wants to know what is going to happen next.

2. Construct your play like a symphony with different paces, combinations of voices and styles to beguile and enchant the ear.

3. Prune well for healthy growth. A German dramatist once said that nine tenths of a writer's work is cutting.

Richard Imison probably read more radio scripts than anybody else in history. He said that from flicking through a script, just looking at the shape of its layout on a succession of pages, he could get an idea of how good the play was going to be. I was sceptical at first, but grew to agree with him. He was talking about what I call the match between music and meaning. The variety of pace, texture, acoustic, of a play both from one scene to another and within each scene is important. Such contrasts can simultaneously beguile the ear and emphasise the message.

One of the many qualities that make Shakespeare a good radio writer is his instinctive realisation of this. He will frequently cut back and forth between poetry and prose, between soliloquy and dialogue, between the interior of a man's mind and a group of characters on battlefield or in the depths of a wood; on a blasted heath or in an orchard; in a grand hall or a dungeon. Each change of acoustic, texture and pace will induce us to prick up our ears.

Remember also that this is the only medium, in which the actors do not learn their parts but in which they pick their speeches off the page. Thus presentation and layout are crucially important and can affect an actor's understanding, feeling and variety of pace.

Similarities with a symphony

Another way to look at the structure of a radio play is to think of it as a musical composition. What is it about a great symphony that enthrals one? There could be as many answers as there are appreciative listeners. It could be the sheer beauty, the power, the amazing variety and contrasts. I should like to suggest that there are two qualities that the structure of a symphony will have in common with the structure of a successful radio play. Firstly there is the variety and contrast between different movements and tempos and between orchestral and solo passages. Secondly the great symphony will continuously delight and surprise, while at the same time seeming to fulfil an expectation on the part of the listener. It is as if in every great work of art there is something that we recognise. Both symphonies and radio plays are a sound continuum that, at their best, will draw us on to a climax, a conclusion that seems inevitable. Each link in the chain will be just right in achieving this end.

A good radio play will be rich in sub-text. The number, the character and the tone of voices will vary from scene to scene and there will be a varied use of sound effects. There can also be music within the scenes. For a really telling contrast in acoustics, some scenes can be recorded in the studio and some on location. Location recording is usually appropriate to naturalistic and particularly to contemporary scenes, whereas studio recording may be better suited to memory or fantasy, in which the participants will call to mind only essential sounds.

Structuring A Play

The beginning of The World Walk

I should like to share with you, in some detail, how Jonathan Smith and I worked very closely together on his stage script of *The World Walk* to make it into a radio play.

The radio version has to attempt to accomplish at least four objectives in the first two minutes.

1. It has to give us some idea of what the play is going to be about. This is accomplished largely by the announcer, but also by Albert Speer's, the central character's, monologue.

2. It has to provide emotional attraction, to help captivate the listener. This is done partly by the choice of music: the Horst Wessel song, a highly evocative Nazi marching tune, that is at once both uplifting and reminiscent of some of the worst atrocities of the Twentieth Century. It is also partly done by the monologue. Although we may already know or be beginning to surmise, that Albert Speer is a convicted Nazi war criminal, we are invited to identify with him and already it is difficult not to feel some sympathy for him.

3. It has to establish the conventions of the play: that we are in for a drama that is both emotional and reflective and that we shall not follow a lineal order of events, but shall jump around as memory and as apprehension dictate. It implies that we shall both be looking back at Albert Speer's past life and forward to his forthcoming release from Spandau Prison.

4. Finally, it has to begin to stimulate some pictures in the listener's mind. Here the monologue is helped by the sound effects, in conveying our hero trudging endlessly round and round a confined space: a different kind of marching, to that which we have just heard behind the Horst Wessel song.

Here are the first two minutes.

ANNOUNCER: 'The World Walk by Jonathan Smith with John Franklyn Robbins as Albert Speer.

<u>FADE UP AND ESTABLISH AN OLD RECORDING OF NAZI SOLDIERS MARCHING TO AND SINGING 'THE HORST WESSEL SONG', FADE DOWN:</u>

ANNOUNCER: 'The World Walk' is based upon the book, 'Spandau, The Secret Diaries' by Albert Speer. The play is set in Spandau prison on September the 30th 1966, but the events range over a thirty year period and do not follow chronological order. Rather, to adapt Wordsworth's idea, they are moments of time recollected in captivity and contemplated until they actually exist again. There is no ordering such thoughts; random, they come, dream-like and real. Imagine such thoughts crowding in on Speer's mind, during the last hours of his imprisonment

<u>SWELL SONG AND THEN SLOWLY CROSSFADE WITH THE SINGLE, SOLITARY, BUT REGULAR FOOTSTEPS OF SPEER ON A GRAVEL PATH. BIRDSONG.</u>

SPEER: (<u>Breathing heavily from his fast pace. He has an anxious, deferential manner</u>) Before I leave I must go and speak to Herr Hess. It won't be easy, I know that, he'll snap at me, but I must. In many ways I'd rather keep at the walk, keep myself to myself, cover a few more kilometres and prepare my mind for tomorrow. I'd rather do anything that keeps me away from that British guard Watkins and his damn fool questions. Ha - there he is near the wash house waiting for me to come round the path with

that smirk on his face and as I pass he'll say,
'Still walking Number Five?'

Answering and posing questions

That took two minutes exactly and the four aims described above
have in the main been achieved.   Hopefully, the listener is
sufficiently enthralled to listen on.   But as well as the promise of
an interesting story unfolding on several levels, there is an
intriguing question forming in the listener's mind: 'What is the
purpose and meaning of this 'world walk' of the title?'.
It is a good idea to both pose and to answer questions. Be careful
that there are not so many questions left unanswered, that the
listener becomes confused and irritated and then switches off.   On
the other hand it is a good idea to have some attractive questions
that make the listener stay with the play in order to discover the
answer.   Too many questions will confuse, while too few will fail
to intrigue the listener.

Sometimes, it can be effective to divulge information to the
listener, while keeping one or two of the main characters in the
dark.   Then the listener has another question; 'What will happen
when the character finds out? How will she or he react?'

The play continues for another minute and a half with
Speer's fast and steady pace and his internal monologue.   In this
passage he mentions, that he also has French, American and
Russian guards. After twenty years of wanting to get out of prison
he is suddenly afraid of his impending release. Will he be able to
face everyone? Will he be able to face leaving the prison with only
Hess left in it: the gravel path, the walls, the garden he has so
lovingly tended?   Also he will miss Anton, the medical orderly
who never made him feel a criminal, who has become a friend.
The thought of Anton makes him stop walking momentarily.
Anton has kept him sane. Sane? Ha! He'd have gone mad without
this garden path to walk round.   He starts trudging again.   Not
that anyone would have called him sane, for walking the distance
from Berlin to Mexico.   And then the guard interrupts:

GUARD: (Bluffly, cheerful cockney) Still walking Number Five?

SPEER: Yes, I have a little more to do.

GUARD: Round and round. The old German discipline, eh? Funny you know, I was only saying to Anton the other day, 'It won't be the same without our Mr. Speer on his rounds!' And I can't think what Anton will do without you to look after.

SPEER: I can't think what I'll do without Anton.

GUARD: So all packed up and ready to go, are we?

SPEER: Yes. Not that I have much to take. Very little. Now if you'll excuse me, I must -

GUARD: (Interrupting) Yeah why not? Keep fit. That's the thing.

SPEER: I must go and say good-bye to Herr Hess.

GUARD: Number Seven? He's over there. Not in a very chatty mood when I last spoke to him. Having one of his off days, Number Seven is, I'd say.

SPEER: Yes, well if you'll excuse me -

GUARD: Before you go, order's just come through. The directors want to see you and Number One at nine o'clock.

SPEER: I was told ten.

GUARD: And I'm telling you nine.

SPEER: Why the change?

GUARD: It was ten o'clock, you're right. But they never agree on anything that lot. Still they wouldn't, would they? I mean, ask yourself: they put one British, one Frenchie, one Russian and one Yank in the same room and they're not likely to get much sense out of them, now are yer? Not that I said that. Still this time in honour of your release the four powers has met and they have at last agreed.

That dialogue lasted exactly one minute and five seconds. Speer marches off.

Changing The Structure: Surprises And Devices

Then, suddenly, in terms of the play's texture we have a contrast and a surprise. Such surprises, as long as they do not confuse, can heighten the listener's interest.

(AND THEN, ABRUPTLY, THE GUARD SPEAKS TO HIMSELF. HE IS A DIFFERENT MAN, QUIET, ANGRY AND BITTER. UNDERNEATH THIS INTRODUCE AN EXTENDED CHORD OF MUSIC TO ADD A QUIETLY SINISTER ATMOSPHERE)

GUARD: (INTERNAL) Go on. Walk till your knee buckles. Walk till your ticker stops and you drop. If I had my way Mr. bloody, smoothy Speer you'd be here a lot longer. And inside your cell. You may have got away with your precious life at Nuremberg, but I'd like to turn the key on you myself, each night, for another twenty years. Yeah, even though it meant seeing you everyday. I'd rather that than seeing you leading them all up the old garden path outside.

(WE LOSE MUSIC AND CUT TO HERR SPEER
TRUDGING TOWARDS HERR HESS. BIRDSONG)

The monologue lasted 32 seconds and the play has lasted so far a total of 5 minutes, 22 seconds. It is worth noting that usually for the same number of words, monologue will usually play more slowly than dialogue.

SPEER: (Approaching) Ah Herr Hess, would you like to join me, for a stroll?

(HESS DOES NOT RESPOND. SPEER HAS ARRIVED)

SPEER: It's a nice evening, Herr Hess and I was wondering if you'd -

HESS: (Interrupts, speaking quickly and angrily) You hoping to get a job as a postman tomorrow, Herr Speer?

The scene continues. So far it is the longest in the play, lasting four and a half minutes. Hess admits that he is feeling malevolent and mischievous today. He taunts Speer about the gaggle of reporters who will be waiting for him and the fact that in the old days at the great Nazi rallies the spotlight was always on Herr Speer.

Now, Herr Hess claims, all the coal delivered to Spandau will be for him alone. He doesn't of course count the scum: the guards and the orderly who look after him.

He taunts Speer with his being a stickler for statistics. Speer has calculated that he has walked 31,936 kilometres. Tomorrow, the day of his release, he will, in his imagination, reach Guadalajara in Mexico. He has hugely admired the Spanish colonial architecture in the Antimarac valley. It is much better, he has the humility to admit than the monumental buildings he designed in the old days as Hitler's Architect in Chief.

They talk particularly of the great Nazi rally of 1937 and of the trouble of erecting the big eagles that Speer designed, how pleased Hitler was with him, and how as he lowered his hand from the salute it fell smack on the bald head of Striecher. Hess roars with laughter.

HESS: The good old days, eh, Herr Speer?

SPEER: (<u>Suddenly coldly angry</u>) Excuse me. I must
                     walk.

Now we are in to one minute of Speer's trudging, monologue, 'The good old days! How could he?!' Has learnt nothing from the past twenty years? 'Calm. I must calm myself. Think of Mexico. Oh no it's that guard again!' He is interrupted

GUARD: Seen the papers, Herr Speer?

And we are into five and a half minutes of dialogue, in which the playwright has the Guard taunt Speer by reading selected passages to him.

GUARD: 'Alone among the prisoners he has fought with
                     all the resources of his lively mind to break
                     through the walls of ignorance around him'.

This device conveys more information about Speer's discipline in prison and his hopes for the future and helps further to reveal the personalities of Speer and of the guard. The guard shows him a picture that must have been taken by telescopic lens. 'If they can photo you from that block of flats over there they could also shoot you Herr Speer'

Introducing New Characters And Moving Through Time

Then Anton, the medical orderly, whose first appearance in the play, we have been anticipating, arrives. Incidentally it can be both more dramatically effective and less confusing to the listeners, if they are already anticipating the introduction of a new character.

Anton tries to rescue Speer from the guard: 'Willy Brandt has sent some flowers to your daughter'. Speer leaves Anton and the guard to argue, as defence and prosecution, about how much in his position as Reichminister for Armaments he was responsible for slave labour.

'Has he not already paid the price? Hasn't he honestly admitted his guilt?' asks Anton. 'If he's so nice how come he was involved with murderers?' taunts the guard. And we are away to Speer and into his mind again. It is marvellous how, if properly signposted, radio can instantaneously and economically change location and perspective, from the exterior world to the inside of somebody's mind.

(TRUDGING ON GRAVEL. SPEER IS BREATHING HARD. TRUDGING STOPS)

SPEER: Can't walk any more... that'll have to do. Damn this heart. I must lie down. At midnight I'll see them all again - Margaret and my children, Hilde, Fritz and my grand children.

For me looking back on this play, twenty five years after I script edited and produced it, I feel this is the first place, where I have a criticism of the script. For the first time, fifteen and a half minutes into the play, the writer, it seems to me, does not manage to convey information without sounding a little artificial or stilted. I am sure Jonathan Smith will forgive me for this criticism. It was his first radio play and as script editor and producer, I should have spotted this and made a constructive suggestion or two.

But then he captures our interest and suspends our disbelief again. He repeats: 'What is the truth?', a question he has asked himself over and over again. 'Who was that young man with my name in 1930, aged twenty five? In 1935, who was that man leaning over the building plans with Hitler? Who was the man, who picked up the telephone in 1942? How did I become involved - how did you become - how did he become - ?' And a little later the guard's question echoes in his mind: 'Just one thing Number Five, how did you become involved with murderers, with anti-Semites?' Suddenly we are projected into the future and we are emerging with Herr Speer from the prison, surrounded by a confusion and cacophony of journalists' questions, culminating in the echoing: 'How does it feel to be free again?'

Thus seventeen and a half minutes into the play, we have what was promised at the beginning: a random moment imagined in captivity, dream-like, yet real enough for Speer. We have momentarily entered the future, Speer's greatest fear. Yet almost immediately, through his memory we escape into Speer's cell, twenty years ago. Clearly signalled and attractively orchestrated, radio can chop about in time as much as you like.

Addressing The Listener

His meditation takes place within his cell. From tomorrow there will only be one prisoner, Herr Hess left. Then after the longest and most effective silence so far in the script (of five seconds), for this thought to sink in, the guards voice intrudes again:

GUARD: (<u>Almost gentle</u>) Close your eyes if you like. Tell us some more, Herr Speer, we're all listening. We want to know.

The play subtly changes its tone. It is as if all the listeners are invited to become Speer's judges.

GUARD: We are not interested in the other prisoners, Herr Speer, we want to know about you.

As writer you need to be careful about how you may choose to address the listener, if you do not wish to break the spell of the story. You can either do so at the beginning, as for example Fay

Weldon does in *The Hole in the Top of the World*, or you can do so more obliquely as Jonathan Smith does here.

SPEER: If you want to understand, I must tell it my way.... from the start... I liked mathematics... I was the best in the school... And rowing, as stroke... directing the crew... with my own rhythm... it was a marvellous feeling you know, leading and co-ordinating... all that power... There wasn't any time for cigarettes, girls... until I met Margaret... And then I remember that day I told Father I wanted to be an architect just like him, and his father. It pleased him and I liked that. We were organisers, architects. It was our tradition. A tradition I brought to shame.

There is a knock on the cell door. It is Anton come to see if all is well, to apologise for the questions of the guard. The guard leaves and Speer more easily pours out his heart to Anton. This is a very long scene in which we flash back again and again to Speer's past. It is Anton's last chance to ask many questions. It seems that he needs to understand as passionately as Speer does. 'Why is that?' we begin to wonder. We feel a small shiver of anticipation.

Gearing Up A Pace

The play takes on a new momentum. Speer was initially more interested in walks in the mountains and in going to the theatre than in politics. But there was poverty all around and although Speer was not exactly poor himself, Hitler seemed to answer a struggling young architect's hopes. He met the great man and we hear the cheering and intoxicating speech making of Hitler's rallies, backed by triumphal Wagnerian music. Hitler employs him as his chief architect. Speer works day and night and hardly sees his family. He is reproached by his father, a gentle, disappointed voice from another era, for being part of a new madness; and by his wife for only being known by the children as 'the man who brings sweets'. We begin to see how the 'good, family man' can become corrupted.

And then we leap forward and we learn of Speer's growing disillusion and we hear his confession to Hess, while walking round the prison garden, of how he planned to kill Hitler. The elements of the play are all working in unison, now, to drive the story forward and unpeel Speer's character layer by layer, so that we, the listeners can share with Speer a better understanding.

After his attempt to kill Hitler failed in late 1944, Speer's vision becomes apocalyptic, like something out of Hieronymus Bosch or Francis Bacon.

SPEER: His skin gradually fell away from his face when
                 he spoke to me and I saw a dark stain right
                 down his body.... And I couldn't see why I had
                 joined the dance. Oh God!

And we flash forward to a few years ago in his cell when it is Anton knocking on the door as he did a few moments previously. It is remarkable how powerful a simple sound effect such as this can be on radio. Anton sees that he is depressed and becomes his saviour, by smuggling extra toilet paper into him.

ANTON: Your leg needs a lot of bandage for a good few
                 months in my medical opinion.

His writing will be hidden there to escape the shredder of the Russian guard. He can begin to seek out the truth; eventually to communicate again with outside world. To a captive this can feel like freedom. (Author's note: I have recently experienced this in helping prisoners to write and produce radio plays). From now on the play becomes more and more free ranging. Speer in prison is on trial, not just from the Guard, from Anton and from his own conscience, but also from his fellow prisoners for admitting too much guilt at his trial by the Allies and thus betraying the ideals of the Nazism; which many of them still maintain.

The author has set up a convention in which he can roam wherever he likes in Speer's life, driven by the overwhelming compulsion to get at the truth - whatever that is. It makes powerful listening.

Anton becomes much more insistent in his questioning, than would seem appropriate for a simple medical orderly. Speer does not appear to be suspicious. He is glad to have an interrogator who is sympathetic and as meticulous for detail as himself. However we, the listeners must begin to become suspicious. This is yet another dramatic device, to keep us listening.

Using Music

About fifty minutes into this ninety-minute play Anton takes his leave, closing the door with a resounding echo and leaving Speer, for the last time, before his release tomorrow, to his solitary soul searching:

SPEER: …But I am a criminal.

                         (INTRODUCE ETHEREAL AND SOOTHING MUSIC
                         UNDER SPEER'S MONOLOGUE)

SPEER: For years I went to the Chapel services. The
                         Chaplain played Bruckner on the gramophone
                         and I moved closer to my family.

                         (THE MOCKING VOICES OF THE FELLOW
                         PRISONERS, ADMIRAL DOENITZ AND HITLER
                         YOUTH LEADER, SCHIRACH INTRUDE)

DOENITZ AND   I should pray, Herr Speer, as much as you

SCHIRACH: can.

                         (THE MUSIC DROWNS THEM OUT AND THEN
                         STOPS)

SPEER: And I tried to pray.

The effect of music cannot be overestimated in radio drama. Here it creates a wonderfully soothing effect. Also Speer himself uses it to blot out his tormentors; but as if he had tried too hard he destroys the music and he is left again, arid, vainly seeking solace, to pray.

One can use music in several ways, but should beware the danger of suddenly seeming to introduce a full piece orchestra into the same setting as the characters. One can establish the convention at the beginning, that music from for a particular symphony or on a particular theme is intrinsic to a central character's emotional make-up. This way the listener will recognise and accept this shorthand whenever it is introduced. Alternatively one can as Speer does here, mention the occasion on which the music is played, and use it to echo in the mind thereafter.

Racing Against The Clock

The play continues with an agonising meeting in prison with his wife Margaret. He is only allowed one minute and ten seconds and a British officer has to be present. She tells him that his mother is paralysed from a stroke; but how she had loved the drawings he had sent her; how she had said he might become a second Durer.

SPEER: When I last saw her, Father shook my hand, but
                    she held back as if I were unclean.

They speak briefly of the children. Margaret tells him that Ernst is having a difficult time at school. And time is up, the interview is over.

It is amazing how skilfully Jonathan Smith manages to invite our insight into and sympathy for this 'good family-man', who became a war criminal, responsible for employing millions in slave labour camps.

Introducing Comedy

In such a relentlessly compelling play, it is important to have moments of comedy. Jonathan Smith provides them. There is the comic outrage of his fellow prisoners when the Prison Chaplain compares them to lepers; and a marvellous scene when the French guard suggests sharing the hundred thousand marks reward for finding the disappeared Nazi criminal, Martin Boorman. Speer decides suddenly to pretend, that really the French guard is Boorman in disguise: the face, the stocky figure, the hair that has been dyed and the French accent, that never really rings true. With wild humour and close to breaking point, he screams around the prison that really Sadot, the French guard, is none other than Martin Boorman!

After the Martin Boorman and the leper incidents, he is silent for weeks, trudging round and round the gardens, keeping sane by meticulously charting his imagined 'World Walk'. He is approaching the Bering Straits between Siberia and Alaska. Often he is accompanied by Hess, who occasionally breaks the silence:

HESS: One of these days they'll make a good technicolour movie about us. (He giggles) Make sure the actor who plays you, Herr Speer, wears a halo.

SPEER: Oh my God! I must have been wandering. I've miscalculated. It's July! The current will have melted everything. We're already out to sea! What am I going to do?

HESS: I'm all right on this ice flow.

This setback to his plans makes him compensate by getting down to frantic writing about the Nazi slave labour plan. He becomes obsessive. He has a weak heart, which we begin to hear beating as more and more questions about the final solution crowd in on him. He falls into a sleep, climaxing in a nightmare, in which, amidst a cacophony of guards' footsteps, slamming cell doors and a litany of the names of the condemned, he thinks the executioners are coming for him.

Reaching The Climax Of The Play

We are nearing the climax of the play. Anton on the last night admits that he was one of Speer's slave labourers. He assumes the role of Speer's judge. 'Let me remind you', he says 'of those films shown at Nuremberg.' We hear the ominous sounding noise of the film running through its spools. The film's calm, measured commentary on the statistics of the dead, interweaves with Anton's interrogation.

Speer's final statement:

SPEER: I am grateful and ashamed of my life. I am
                    ashamed and grateful for my imprisonment.
                    And now if you will excuse me I must walk a
                    little.

The guard's final statement, in reply to the releasing officer:

GUARD: If he was the best of the bunch, he must have
                    been the worst.

The play ends with Speer being released from the prison gates to be met by the full force of the paparazzi. Whether or not this is true freedom and whether or not Albert Speer has expiated his guilt is left for us, the listeners, to decide.

Since he wrote this first play Jonathan Smith has gone on to write many successful radio plays. As we go to press his most recent *The Last Bark of the Bulldog* about the last years of Winston Churchill, has just been nominated for the Sony Award. You can learn more on the very interesting website http://web.ukonline.co.uk/suttonelms/JS.HTML

We have spent a long time on *The World Walk*, this single, ninety minute play, but hopefully this analysis will help to cast light on many of the points made in the rest of the book. The analysis was intentionally more thorough at the beginning, where the playwright was putting together the elements and establishing the conventions that he would use again and again throughout the play.

Hopefully one day it will be possible to record a new production of this play, which you the listener might download from the Internet.

4 Exploring Language and Belief

Using Words As Flying Sculptures

This chapter is not about the connection between conventional religious belief and language, but about how language properly employed can make the listener participate and believe in a reality beyond the mundane and the every day. The power of speech can invest the ordinary and familiar experiences of life with humour, meaning, grief, joy and enchantment that we might not otherwise glimpse.

The most ancient form of story telling, aeons before the invention of writing, was that of the oral tradition. The earliest story tellers, through their skill and their magic, would conjure up pictures that cave dwellers would see in the flames of the fire that kept them war7m at night and which kept away wild animals. Druid storytellers would memorise by heart thousands of lines of narrative verse. As late as Shakespeare's day most story telling was by word of mouth and his audience were far more sensitive to the nuances and resonances of the human voice than we are in this, our literary and our visual age. Indeed it was most unusual to read 'silently' before the Victorian era.

D.G. Bridson, a radio drama producer in the forties and fifties, pointed out in his memoir, *Prospero and Ariel*, that, 'Not many of us can teach ourselves to write until we teach ourselves to talk'. His contemporary, Donald McWhinnie suggested how we should prepare to listen to radio: 'Sit in a dark room and talk and listen. Even if you are not vitally interested in words, they suddenly acquire a compulsion of meaning, they did not have before; they develop a richness of texture through being isolated, and you focus your sensibility and imagination on them as you rarely do in daylight'.

The French poet, Paul Claudel, employed a vivid image to describe this tangible power. For him a word was made by mouthed gestures. He talked of the breath of life, 'inspired' or breathed into us by God. This we in turn 'expire' in the form of vowels shaped with our lips, tongue and teeth to form consonants and so we model words; which we expel into the air in the form of 'flying sculptures.' This is a wonderfully French conceit, but one that echoes in my mind when I hear poetry really well delivered. Many years ago I had the privilege of producing Paul Scofield reading Gerard Manley Hopkins' *The Wreck Of The Deutschland*:

> Thou mastering me
> God! giver of breath and bread;
> World's strand, sway of the sea;
> Lord of living and dead;
> Thou hast bound bones and veins in me, fastened me flesh,
> And after it almost unmade, what with dread
> Thy doing: and dost thou touch me afresh?
> Over again I feel thy finger and find thee.

This and the twenty-five subsequent stanzas were a magnificent procession of flying sculptures!

Understanding What The Word Has To Accomplish

In radio, as writer, you will need to be, at the same time, both more economical and more imaginative than you would be on the page. A reader can skim through paragraphs of description. He can put down and pick up the book, ruminate and recap. None of this can happen in the continuum of a radio play. Even on cassette or CD it is inconvenient. Thus you will need to learn to describe scenery and people and to express depth of feeling, implicitly and obliquely and in a matter of seconds.

Giles Cooper does so in this excerpt from *Without the Grail*. In a few sentences he establishes an atmosphere of heat and exhaustion, vividly paints the locale where most of the action is to take place, carries his plot a stage forward, gives a new insight into his leading character - and at the same time diverts us with humour and suspense. The writing is pared to the bone. When performed it is rich in overtones.

(FADE IN CAR RUNNING: IT SLOWS AND STOPS).

(PAUSE.)

INNES: What's the matter?

INDIAN DRIVER: Stop to cool the engine.

INNES: Okay, you're the driver. (PAUSE.) So this is the jungle.

DRIVER: Yes, all jungle here.

INNES: H'm - Very dusty looking.

DRIVER: The road is making it dusty. Inside is green.

(PAUSE.)

INNES: There's a railway line over there. Where does it go?

DRIVER: No place. Into the jungle, stop.

INNES: Eh? - Why?

DRIVER: Military reasons. Now abandoned.

INNES: Wartime?

DRIVER: Yes, wartime. In Assam there were armies all the time. Now in the jungle here live all things.

INNES: Er - animals, you mean?

DRIVER: No, *things*. Wheels and chains gone rusting. Old guns and tanks not moving. In one place were fifty thousand teeth-brush, abandoned. All abandoned.

(PAUSE.)

(CAR STARTS AND MOVES OFF. FADE OUT.)

The car tells us that we are moving in and out of the scene. The rest is done by language.

Releasing The Poetry From Your Prose

At the risk of sounding academic, I should like to examine why in *Julius Caesar* after the assassination of Caesar, Shakespeare has Brutus address the Roman crowd in prose and Anthony address them in poetry. I first approached this question practically, through directing drama students. I surmised that Shakespeare made this distinction, because prose is more tentative and lacks the authority, the confidence and the natural beauty of poetry. He knew that poetry would be more persuasive and powerful and would help Anthony to captivate and convince the Roman populace, at the expense of Brutus and of Cassius.

In a sense much excellent spoken prose contains elements of poetry and in my thirty or so years working with writers, I have come to the romantic conclusion that each of us has an 'original and unique voice'; a sense of poetry waiting to be unlocked. Once or twice I have been rewarded by hearing writers develop from the mundane, prosaic and stilted and take wings with original, beautiful and arresting language. They have found their voice.

You, as a writer, having accomplished this have to help the actor to lift it off the page and in this respect I should like to give you a tip that I learnt from Peter Tinniswood. I noticed in the first script of his that I worked on, that he had set it out in a particular way. He was gratified when I spotted this. I promised that the BBC typist would reflect the same lay out in the production script.

Here is an example of what I mean from the beginning of his award winning play, *The Village Fete*:

NANCY: [TO MIKE].
We moved from London to the country on a misty morning in early May.
There were no blackheaded gulls.
Thrushes sang.
Next door neighbour's cat howled.
And the house spider came out from his hole by the fireplace in the drawing-room to bid us all good-bye.
He seemed so smug about it all.
The removal men couldn't park outside the house.
But, of course.
William got distraught.
But, of course.

WILLIAM: [ALOUD] It's so outrageously inconvenient.

ROSIE: Moving house is always inconvenient, William.

WILLIAM: But it's specifically inconvenient to me, Rosie.
I'm approaching the climax of my book.
It's all locked away in my head.
I am rapidly approaching the denouement.
Do you understand?
The denouement.
And this move will destroy it.

The actor has to work very fast. He has to lift the words off the page, deliver them, monitor how he is saying them and attempt to make them even more spontaneous, truthful and interesting. The actors have to listen to each other and use each other's energy. They have to respond to each other's pitch, timing and tone. The lay out on the page is crucial. Peter Tinniswood's trick of the trade certainly helps.

Working Without Visual Aids

See how many pictures there were in this passage from *The Village Fete*. Compare it with this passage from Timothy West's wonderful spoof on how *not* to write a radio play: *This Gun That I Have In My Right Hand Is Loaded*.

LAURA: What's that you've got under your arm, Clive?

CLIVE: It's an evening paper, Laura.
       (<u>PAPER NOISE</u>)

I've just been reading about the Oppenheimer smuggling case. Good gracious, it's nice to sit down after that long train journey from the insurance office in the city.

LAURA: Let me get you a drink, Clive darling.

       (<u>LENGTHY POURING, CLINK</u>)

CLIVE: Thank you, Laura my dear.

       (<u>CLINK, SIP, GULP</u>)

       Aah, Amontillado eh? Good stuff. What are you having?

LAURA: I'll think I'll have a whisky, if it's all the same to you.

       (<u>CLINK, POURING, SYPHON</u>)

CLIVE: Whisky, eh? That's a strange drink for an attractive, auburn-haired girl of twenty-nine anything wrong?

LAURA: No, it's nothing, Clive, I -

CLIVE: Yes?

LAURA: No, really, I -

CLIVE: You're my wife, Laura. Whatever it is you can
                tell me. I'm your husband.

This may be a grossly unfair comparison, but it can illustrate some useful points. Peter Tinniswood's passage of almost exactly as many words has many more interesting, original and beautiful images. I count at least nine in Nancy's first speech. How exactly a house spider can look smug, I am not sure, but my imagination is working on it. Not only are there far fewer images in *This Gun…*, but they are spelt out in an (intentionally) stilted and clumsy way.

Colin Haydn Evans in his book, *Writing for Radio*, said that if you want to understand how radio drama works listen to as many bad radio plays as possible. In good plays it is sometimes difficult to see the sleight of hand by which it is done; to see where the seams are. If you listen to bad plays, you can see that the technique shows all too transparently and you can see what not to do. No doubt when he came to write this script, Timothy West had worked on too many radio plays that creaked; in which the writers had not mastered the art of obliquely drawing pictures.

Anyway, I recommend that you listen to as many radio plays as possible. You will hear both good and bad.

Suspending Disbelief

I should now like to give you an illustration from *Of The Levitation At St. Michael's* by Carey Harrison, a play, that both portrays something, you have probably never seen and that also should help you to suspend disbelief in such a phenomenon. It is two-hander about a couple of goat keepers in East Anglia. One of them, Elizabeth, acts as the narrator:

ELIZABETH: We were going on an errand of mercy, to
                examine a sick goat owned by a novice
                goatkeeper. A passion for goats was about the
                only thing I shared in common with Matty;
                that, and the sheer pleasure of getting away,

from time to time. For an hour or two. Matty had a husband, Ted; a backward child - to be precise, a Mongol child - called Winston; and the finest herd of goats in East Anglia.

MATTY CAN BE HEARD, STOMPING THROUGH THE MUD TOWARDS ELIZABETH'S CAR, MUTTERING DARKLY

ELIZABETH: I had a husband: Jack. No children. One or two reasonably good goats. Prize-winners.

After a dialogue scene as they set off in the car, she continues:

ELIZABETH: We were an unlikely pair, to tell the truth. But livestock brings people together across all sorts of social barriers. And - temperamental ones too. Matty and I were very different kinds of goatkeeper. She was a goat breeder; a pro. I was an amateur. Encouraged by my husband. Though not out of love. Years ago when Jack first stood for Parliament, the local television people came and filmed me milking a goat - at Jack's request. The common touch, to impress the locals.

Later Matty and Elizabeth, having lost the address, of where they are supposed to be going, end up visiting a remote Ghilbertine Abbey chapel instead.   It is this passage that invites the listener to suspend disbelief in a seemingly supernatural phenomenon.

MATTY: Well it's a lovely place. It makes you *want* to pray.

            (MATTY MEANS NOTHING OF THE KIND; SHE CERTAINLY DOESN'T FIND IT 'LOVELY'; AS ELIZABETH IS WELL AWARE. A MOMENT'S PAUSE)

Incidentally this direction, about how the words should be delivered, is skilfully placed in the script. If such a chunk came within the speech, it might deflect the actor, momentarily but crucially, from making the line her own and from getting the timing right. A single word's direction as in the next speech is not such a problem, though even here it is a good idea not to bombard the actor with too many notes (both on and off the page!). My advice would only be to give 'how to interpret' instructions, when it is not obvious to the intelligent and intuitive actor.

Elizabeth in turn suggests that Matty might say a prayer, but soon regrets her suggestion.

MATTY: Pray for Winston? That wouldn't do much
                good, would it. He's going to die soon - you
                know that. They all do. They don't often reach
                thirty.

ELIZABETH: Yes - I didn't really mean that, Matty -

MATTY: What then? Just - put in a word for him, seeing
                he'll be coming up for judgement shortly. Is
                that it? Almighty God: remember Winston.

                (ELIZABETH SAYS NOTHING)

MATTY: What? Remember Winston?

ELIZABETH: I'm sure he does.

MATTY: What? I should think He *does*! If anyone
                bloody sent him into the world, He did. He
                knows! If He was going to *do* something about
                it - He won't need to be reminded, will He!

                (AS MATTY'S VOICE RISES, THE ECHOES BOOM
                AROUND THE WALLS)

ELIZABETH: (Cowed) No, of course not.

MATTY: *What* then? What am I supposed to do, then? Ask for something? Pray for something? Anything I want at all? Send me a helper, Lord. Another idiot. Just for a lark send me a bloody half-wit for a husband. Oh *He knows*!

(A MOMENT'S PAUSE)

MATTY: Shall I give him the pleasure, then? Come on, you tell me! What do I say? Thank you Lord for giving me a monster, for choosing me, thank you wonderful LORD. Is that it? Thank you sweet Jesus, it's your chosen mother speaking -

(AS MATTY RANTS, MUSIC RETURNS, ONE HELD NOTE, SWELLING)

ELIZABETH: (CLOSE; TO US) She was lit up with rage, appalling.

MATTY: Do you think he wants me crawling back for help? Do you? Now? When I've had twenty years of it? Do you? Please God! He'd bloody laugh at me! (Self-mocking) O Lord - thank you for picking me, what did I do, did I offend You? (Thunderously) Offend me? Ha ha ha you silly woman!

ELIZABETH: (CLOSE, AS THE NOTE SWELLS) Then it happened. Then it began: quite gradually. Oh, it was comic at first, her fat little body there in the middle of an aisle; lifting up into the air. Matty floating in mid-air. But the laughter stuck in my throat. By the time she was fully two foot off the ground, all I could do was gape. Her voice had trailed away. How long had we been silent?

I was staring. She was looking down; mouth open, silent. Fat little legs; not swinging; stiff. I saw it clearly. I felt dizzy. Then she spoke.

(MATTY'S VOICE COMES, HOARSE, FRIGHTENED)

MATTY: Help - me -

(THE NOTE STILL HOLD, HIGH IN THE AIR)

ELIZABETH: I rose to help her. Did I rise?

(A HEAVY SOUND: SOMEONE FALLING. THE NOTE BREAKS OFF. FOOTSTEPS; RUNNING. MATTY'S VOICE, HARSH, COMING CLOSER, AS SHE RUNS OVER TO ELIZABETH

MATTY: Elizabeth! Elizabeth!

(SILENCE. THE ECHOES FADE. THE OUTDOOR ACOUSTIC RETURNS. BREATHING; PANTING)

ELIZABETH: Stop.

MATTY: What's the matter?

ELIZABETH: It's my hat. I've left my hat inside. My woolly hat. It must have fallen off.

MATTY: Come on, then. We'll go back.

ELIZABETH: Alright

(HER TONE MAKES MATTY PAUSE)

MATTY: You still look a bit queer. You stay. I'll go back and fetch it.

ELIZABETH: No. Leave it.

MATTY: What? That's a nice hat.

ELIZABETH: Leave it.

MATTY: You just want to leave it there? (<u>A MOMENT'S
                PAUSE. SHE TUTS MILDLY</u>) some people -
                that's a nice hat.

ELIZABETH: Did I black out, or what? I must have fainted.

MATTY: You fainted alright. Passed clean out.

ELIZABETH: Matty.. what happened?

MATTY: I sat you up. You came round fast enough.

ELIZABETH: Before I fainted. What happened?
MATTY: (<u>Blandly</u>) *I* don't know dear. It was most
                peculiar, *I* can tell you.

ELIZABETH: You were. (<u>She chokes on a nervous laugh</u>) you
                were - sort of floating.

MATTY: (<u>As before</u>) Was I? I can remember looking
                down. It scared me for a moment. Everything
                looked different. Stretched.

ELIZABETH: Stretched?

MATTY: I was floating was I? How d'you mean?

ELIZABETH: Above the ground.

MATTY: Floating above the ground. No wonder
                everything looked funny.

(<u>ABRUPTLY MATTY BREAKS INTO A RAUCOUS
CHUCKLE</u>)

MATTY: It's a bloody miracle, then.

I have quoted from this play at some length, because I should like you to think about the structure. The author has not introduced us to the world of the supernatural at the beginning. On the contrary, we have inhabited a naturalistic world of amused scepticism. However because of the contrasting attitudes of the two characters - of disbelief at what she has seen on Elizabeth's part and of dismissal on Matty's - I think the author plays a clever confidence trick on the listener. The listener is drawn into the situation and probably accepts, that Matty *really* has been suspended in the air.

Carey Harrison has returned to a similar theme in many of his plays. In *Moving Statues,* his radio comedy about an Irish wedding, the only guest who sees the statue of the Virgin moving is also the only unbeliever at the wedding. The believers on the other hand long to see a sign, but are not vouchsafed the seeing of a miracle. This is a nice use of irony and of paradox to help suspend disbelief in the listener.

It reminds me of the story of the French novelist and fervent atheist Emil Zola, who claimed that, if he saw a miraculous cure at Lourdes, he would believe. He visited the shrine and saw Solange, a small girl on the point of death, being instantaneously and inexplicably cured; but he had to admit that what he saw with his own eyes still did not make him believe.

My advice when writing a play or compiling a feature about religion or spirituality is to attempt to attract both believers and sceptics. Leave the listener to make her mind. Let her be the judge.

5 Using Scenes, Music, Sound Effects and Silence

Defining A Radio Scene

There are two ways of defining scenes in radio: from the listener's and from the producer's point of view. For the listener a new scene happens, when there is a change of location or a shift in time. It may for example be a shift from first person narration to a dialogue during a storm at sea, or a flashback from a mother and daughter talking today to the mother and her mother talking twenty five years ago.

From the director's point of view a scene will be a chunk of the play that is convenient to record in one go and, as a director, I will often mark up the author's script in this way, to make clear my intentions to the technicians. However I will be as careful as I can never to meddle with the author's intentions.

Beginning And Ending A Radio Scene

The opening scenes of Fay Weldon's play, *Polaris*, alternate between the interior of a submarine and the home of Meg, the pregnant wife of one of the naval officers. I shall give you a couple of ins and outs from one scene to another, showing how the next scene is set up, using language, music and sound effects in an entertaining and economic way. This is how the play starts:

> (WE ARE IN THE CONTROL ROOM OF A POLARIS
> SUBMARINE, IN DOCK, ON THE SURFACE. THE
> CAPTAIN AND JIM, THE FIRST LIEUTENANT, ARE
> COMPLETING A DAILY-USER CHECK, AND
> EXCHANGING A MURMURED CONVERSATION
> OVER ASSORTED WHIRRS, CLICKS AND THE
> SOUND OF RADIO 1: 'RUDOLPH THE RED NOSED
> REINDEER'. THE CAPTAIN IS A SUAVE AND

EASY FELLOW: RATHER TOO MUCH SO FOR HIS
FIRST LIEUTENANT.

CAPTAIN: Hydroplane system. One-man-control?

JIM: A OK sir

CAPTAIN: Plotting tables?

JIM: All complete, sir

CAPTAIN: Sounder?

JIM: Hold on, sir

(SILENCE. THEN PING-PING-PING FROM THE
ECHO SOUNDER)

JIM: A OK sir

(THAT SEEMS TO BE THAT. THE PLAY PROPER,
AS IT WERE, BEGINS)

Let us skip forward to the ending of the first and the beginning of
the second scene:

JIM: Cold out there, sir. Snug as a bug in here.

CAPTAIN: Snug as a bug. User check complete. Down
                  periscope. Goodbye, God's eye. See you in
                  three months. Take care. Small you said
                  (referring to Tim, the Navigator's wife), and
                  learning to be sensible. Ah!

(RADIO 4: 'DECK THE HALLS WITH FERNS AND
HOLLY')

CAPTAIN: She won't be lonely?

JIM: They have a dog.

(CUT TO: THOMPSON, THE DOG, HALF
SPRINGER, HALF ALSATIAN, WHICH MAKES
HIM AMIABLE AND ENORMOUS, SLURPS AND
GRUNTS OVER THE SLEEPING MEG'S FACE. THE
BEDSIDE RADIO IS TUNED TO RADIO 4 AND
CONTINUES FROM THE PREVIOUS SCENE IN THE
NEW ACOUSTIC. RADIO 4: 'TIS THE SEASON TO
BE JOLLY')

THOMPSON: Phloph

MEG: Go away Thompson. Get off this bed. You're
                 not allowed on the bed. Get off! Timmy, get
                 him off . Timmy? Oh, Timmy, you're gone. I
                 forgot. Three months. Oh Thompson, you
                 stupid dog, what will I do? Sleep. 'Tis the
                 season to be jolly.'

Thus Fay Weldon invents some call signs to signal, where we are
going: the ping ping of the echo sounder, the Christmas songs on
Radios 1 and 4 and the slobbering of Thompson. This is the next
scene change:

POSTMAN: You're too isolated up here. You'd have done
                 better to have chosen nearer to the Base with
                 the others. But that's your affair.

                 (HE GOES)

MEG: I didn't want to be near the others. I wanted us
                 all alone, just the two of us. Oh, Timmy.
                 'God rest you, merry gentlemen,
                 Let nothing you dismay.'

                 (THOMPSON JOINS IN, HOWLING)

Be quiet, Thompson, you stupid dumb dog. If you could talk there'd be some point to you.

(SLIGHT EDGE OUT. DOWN IN THE POLARIS: PING-PING-PING)

CAPTAIN: 'God rest you, merry gentlemen,
                 Let nothing you dismay' –
                 Glad to see you, Timmy. Now perhaps we can
                 get on with the fast cruise.

TIMMY: Morning, sir. I was last aboard. That's never
                 happened before.

CAPTAIN: You've never been married before.
                 'Remember Christ our Saviour
                 Was born on Christmas day' -

It is interesting how Fay Weldon uses different characters listening to the same radio programme to link the scenes.

In the next example, the writer plays with the ambiguity of similarly sounding words. Within a half hour comedy of five scenes, the playwright starts three of them with different meanings of the same sound.

(INDONESIAN GAMELAN MUSIC ON LOVE'S AND FLO'S HI FI SYSTEM)

ANNOUNCER: We present 'A To B and Back Again' by Nick
                 Pullin with Christian Rodska as Love and Liz
                 Goulding as Flo.

MIX MUSIC INTO SCENE 1: LOVE'S LOUD SIPPING AND SLURPING HIS DRINK.

LOVE: Wales!

FLO: North - or like south?

LOVE:	North. I mean there's fewer people. Less cars.
FLO:	That's right.
LOVE:	I mean, can't you just see all that clean air? You know.
FLO:	I know.
LOVE:	I mean, we could get a goat. (*and so on*)

SCENE 3   ALSO STARTS WITH GAMELAN MUSIC AND LOVE SLURPING

FLO:	Whales?
LOVE:	Oh, yeah
FLO:	What like..
LOVE:	Migrating. They swim past the coast every year. Hump backs, blues, sperm.
FLO:	Oh - is it clean? (*and so on*)

SCENE 4. DIDGEREEDOO MUSIC ON HI FI SYSTEM AND LOVE SLURPING

KEV:	Wails!
LOVE:	What?
KEV:	Wails! He's on my lap, right. And he just sits there and wails. Cries his bloody eyes out.

The repetition of words of the same or similar sound is not unlike the use of music to link scenes.

Using Music In Radio Drama

Perhaps the most obvious use of music in radio drama is in a play about a composer's life. Playwright, Bruce Stewart, began *Symphonic Variations* about the elderly Cesar Franck's love for the young Irish composer, Augusta Holmes, with one of the most romantic pieces of music ever written. Being a married man and a strict Catholic, Franck poured his passion into a composition, that was not at all his usual style. In that way he sublimated, what might otherwise have become an adulterous affair.

(THE BEGINNING OF THE FIRST MOVEMENT OF CESAR FRANCK'S PIANO QUINTET. AFTER 15 SECONDS FADE AND KEEP UNDER HIS MONOLOGUE)

CESAR: Oh my soul! My love! Only in music shall I reach out to you. Only in music shall we become as one. We shall identify, conjoin, like light from the far stars, shining, enduring, as long as music itself. My soul, my love, my Augusta!

(SWELL MUSIC)

Music can be used in many ways. It can swing you instantaneously from one mood to another. It can - as subtly as a raised eyebrow - give to a phrase an extra, and possibly contradictory, level of meaning. It can provide unity, where unity may otherwise be difficult to achieve. Simple counterpoint, perhaps using one instrument, like the zither in Carol Reed's *The Third Man*, can be very effective.

I should like to give you an example that with the appropriate texts and compact discs you can try out for yourself. Such preparation is your responsibility as a radio playwright. I have twice produced *A Midsummer Night's Dream* with the students of the Bristol Old Vic Theatre School for local radio. I had in mind Chesterton's description; that the play is about 'the mysticism of happiness'. On each occasion, I chose French romantic music that seemed admirably to convey this sentiment.

I am strict with the students over the delivery of the verse. If the actor gets the metre and the timing right, then the pictures and the emotion and the meaning come alive. I fed the music to the actors through earphones, so that it would not be picked up by the microphone. This meant I could fine tune and adjust the levels in post production. I said to them, 'This is giving you the emotional content. However I want you to counterpoint the rhythm, so that you really strive to be faithful to Shakespeare's verse'. The experiment proved more successful, than I had imagined.

At the time of my first production I still had Cesar Franck's *Piano Quintet* echoing in my mind. I first introduced it to help exaggerate Helena's unrequited longing for Demetrius. Having established this convention, I used the same piece of music as the lovers' theme at several crucial points. The greater the pangs of love, the greater the comedy:

<u>(ESTABLISH FRANCK'S PIANO QUINTET AND THEN FADE BUT KEEP UNDER THE SPEECH)</u>

HELENA: How happy some o'er other some can be!
            Through Athens I am thought as fair as she.
            But what of that? Demetrius thinks not so…
            (*and so on*)

We kept it, softly, under the whole speech and swelled it at the end.

I wanted to do something similar with the fairies and was fortunate to find a marvellous CD collection of music for oboe and guitar. This gave me a unity for the fairies and for the royal couple, who are to be wedded. I chose Jacque Ibert's *Entr'acte* for Peaseblossom and for Puck. Ibert is a delicate and witty composer and this piece has the right quicksilver quality:

PEASEBL'M: Over hill, over dale,
            Thorough bush, thorough brier,
            Over park, over pale,
            Thorough flood, thorough fire,

> I do wander every where,
> Swifter than the moon's sphere...

Then for Titania's and Oberon's famous confrontation:

OBERON: I'll met by moonlight, proud Titania.

TITANIA: What, jealous Oberon! Fairies, skip hence;
       I have forsworn his bed and company.

OBERON: Tarry, rash wanton; am not I thy lord...?

I chose Erik Satie's *Gnossienne No. 1*. To my ear it has the stateliness of a royal dance, while at the same time possessing something both whimsical and threatening. I also found a regal and mysterious piece called *La Romanesca* by Fernando Sor. This I used as the title music, to go behind the credits and to introduce the court of Theseus. Finally for the mechanicals, Bottom, Quince and the gang I had some gifted and inventive students form a skiffle band and improvise their own comic music.

Music can be a wonderful shorthand in introducing and reminding us of an emotion, a character or a picture. The more thought, the writer gives to it, the more the director has to build upon. Sometimes one may be able to afford a composer and some instrumentalists. Most broadcasting companies have an agreement with the Performing Rights Society, whereby they are authorised to use excerpts from commercial recordings of music. If however you are selling your script to a CD or cassette distributor, you will need to be very careful about the copyright laws. The initial expense of having your music specially composed and performed may pay off in the long run.

Using Sound Effects

The theatre director, Tyrone Guthrie, wrote several radio plays. He said the writer should be responsible for the entire sound pattern. In his play *The Flowers Are Not For You To Pick* he described the sound of a non-naturalistic sea: 'By its rhythms and tone it may be possible to suggest not merely the water in which our hero is engulfed, but the beating of the heart, the tumult of fear, the immutable laws and irresistible strength of nature compared with our puny and inconstant selves.' I can imagine the creative composer Elizabeth Parker, late of the BBC's Radiophonic Workshop, rising to such a challenge.

Most sound effects are far more straightforward than this. I suggest to writers that they should be minimal. As Matisse, in the outlines of his drawing, leaves the viewer to fill in the content and the greater picture, so the radio playwright should give the listener just enough to trigger the imagination.

The greatest number of complaints that one receives from listeners are about plays, that are swamped by sound effects or by a level of music that drowns out the nuances of language. I remember Peter Tinniswood, in an actor's narration, writing: 'WINSTON KNOCKED ON THE DOOR'. An over enthusiastic and literal-minded studio manager provided the sound effect of knocking on a studio door. Peter and I asked, 'What are you doing? It's already there in the listener's head. Let's only have the sound effect of the door opening, before the dialogue commences'. Incidentally I generally hate doors in radio plays. I usually ask writers to lose all openings and closings, that are not vital for information or for dramatic effect. On the other hand, I like to have fun with sound effects. In Carey Harrison's *I Never Killed My German* there is a moment when we hear the sound, of what could be tapping on a hollow wooden box. Then:

WILLY: (NARRATING) "It's all in there," I said, tapping my brainbox....

Thus a rather hollow head is evoked. The American radio drama director, Tony Palermo, arrives by a different route at a similar conclusion to mine. He writes:

"A sound effects artist will always grab a device and then manipulate it. So model your cues to follow that same process. Indicate what the sound is first, then how it is to be played---and for how long. Think NOUN---> VERB----> MODIFIER." In production, this style of cue makes performance easier, but if the writer thinks this way, then cast and director also benefit from the clarity. I also suggest that writers limit their use of SFX to what they would hear in their head when they read a scene from a book. Too much sound is just noise--even if it is realistic to the location or action. I avoid confusion--or lulling sound beds. Clarity is all."

Using Silence

How long you hold a pause; how you fade in and out of scenes; how long you give the listener to form an image in his mind or digest a thought or feeling or to anticipate the next scene can be very important. Comparative silence, that is how you travel from full volume to absolute silence and back again, is an important part of a writer's armoury. On when to have music or when to have silence, Tony Palermo writes:

> "If you can't find exactly the right music for a scene, try using just something to "cleanse the palate" between scenes and allow the audience to rest their ears."

One of the most powerful moments of *earned* silence that I have achieved as a director was in a performance by Walter Matthau of Fay Weldon's *The Hole in the Top of the World:* "Silence is frightening". See page 30 above.

6 Character and Comedy

Deciding How Many Characters?

This is a question I am often asked by newcomers to radio drama. There are four points to bear in mind:

1. The listener will only 'see' characters, if they are described or if they are identified by speaking or being spoken to. It is no good putting in the directions, that a character is present in a scene or sequence and expecting the listener to read the writer's mind; to know this by magic.

2. It is easy to confuse the listener by having too many characters in a scene. If you read the following (abridged) excerpt from *This Gun That I Have In My Left Hand Is Loaded* and try to see and commit to memory all the characters introduced, I think you will take my point.

(<u>FADE IN PUB NOISES</u>)

HAWKINS: (<u>Middle-aged, cheerful Londoner</u>) Evening, Mabel. Busy tonight, isn't it.

BARMAID: It certainly is, Mr. Hawkins. I've been on my feet all evening.

FARRELL: (<u>APPROACHING, MIDDLE-AGED, CHEERFUL LONDONER</u>) Evening, George, what are you having?

HAWKINS: A pint of the usual, please.

FARRELL: Two pints of the usual, please, Mabel.

BARMAID: (<u>OFF</u>) Coming up, Mr. Farrell.

HAWKINS: Evening, Norman

JACKSON:	(MIDDLE-AGED, CHEERFUL, LONDONER) Hello there George. What are you having, Bert?
FARRELL:	I'm just getting them, Norman.
JACKSON:	Well, leave me out I'm getting one for Charlie Illingworth. Two halves of the usual, Mabel.
BAINES:	(COMING UP, MIDDLE-AGED, CHEERFUL, LONDONER) Evening all.
JACKSON:	Hello, Arnold, haven't seen you in ages.
BARMAID:	Your change, Mr. Farrell
FARRELL:	Thanks, Mabel. Where's Charlie got to? Ah, there you are, Charlie. You know Arnold Baines, don't you?
ILLING:	(CHEERFUL, LONDONER, MIDDLE-AGED) Known the old so-and- so for ages. What'll you have?
JACKSON:	No, no, I'm getting them. What is it?
BAINES:	Oh, I'll just have my usual, thanks.
JACKSON:	Who's looking after you, George, old man?
BARMAID:	There's yours, Mr. Hawkins.
MR HAWKINS:	Bung ho!
FARRELL: BAINES:	Cheers, George. Cheers, Norman.
JACKSON:	Cheers, Bert
ILLING:	Cheers, Arnold.

3. Just as in language you need to be as economical as you can, to allow each speech to accomplish as many functions as possible; so I recommend most writers to have as few characters as they absolutely need. This will save on the production budget; but, more importantly, listeners will tend to be more interested in and to identify with characters, who develop throughout a play and who appear in more than one scene. I sometimes suggest to aspiring writers that they should combine two relatively minor characters into one more rounded and interesting character.

4. Again the fewer characters you have within a play, the more there will be for each actor to get his teeth into. Although this may mean that there are fewer parts overall, at least those actors that are in work should have a more fulfilling time.

While on the subject of actors, I think it can be a very useful exercise for a playwright to write a short biography and background of each of his characters. This can be helpful in providing insight and interpretation for the director and actors, who have to work very fast in radio. It may also help you, the playwright, to gain insight into and to provide richness and sub-text for your characters.

Why Character and Comedy?

I believe, that in radio drama, the revealing of character and what it is that moves the listener to laughter have much in common. I first came to the conclusion, that the best radio comedy takes the form of a gradual recognition on the part of the listener, many years ago, when I produced a series of autobiographical comedies by the probation officer and journalist, Geoffrey Parkinson. They are the most appealing and compassionate kind of comedy, in which the subject laughs at himself.

My favourite, *The Non-conforming Non-conformist*, is about how Geoffrey, as an adolescent in the 1950's, loses an over-literal faith as a member of the Sutton Methodist Youth Club and how he finds - or rather tries to find - girls. I shall give four excerpts; the first to show you how the play starts:

RUMBUSTIOUS INTRODUCTION ON THE
CHAPEL HARMONIUM.

GEOFFREY: (NARRATING) I was first taken to church
                  when I was six years old

THE CONGREGATION START SINGING ROUSING
EVANGELICAL HYMN. TAKE DOWN BEHIND.

GEOFFREY: Our family had its own pew. My grand father
                  sat with formidable dignity at the first place just
                  by the aisle; next to him, more relaxed, came
                  my father. Then my mother, my elder brother,
                  John and finally me.   I thought I behaved
                  rather well in church, but nobody else shared
                  this view. Complaints started with my grand
                  father and made their way along the pew.
                  BRING UP HYMN AGAIN FOR A MOMENT

GRAND-:   Tell Geoffrey not to fidget so much.
FATHER

FATHER: Oh yes. Claire, tell Geoffrey to behave himself.

MOTHER: Yes dear. John, would you ask Geoffrey to try
                  and sit still. It's not for much longer.

JOHN: Okay. (Loud Whisper) Geoff!

YOUNG GEOFF: Yes?

JOHN: Shut up mucking around.

YOUNG GEOFF: I'm not doing anything.

JOHN: Shut up!

SWELL HYMN AND FADE

The play continues with Geoffrey frequently confused by religion. Even those of us, who have not had a formal religious upbringing, will recognise the wonderful confusions that grown ups can lead children into. Geoffrey Parkinson had the innocence to take such matters literally at the time, and the talent, later in life, to distil such experiences in his writing. For example, on one occasion his mother explained, how they did not touch fermented liquor in their family and his father explained how many homes had been ruined by drink.

YOUNG GEOFF: Why did Jesus turn water into wine then?

MOTHER: Oh, I'm sure it wasn't real wine, Geoffrey. It
               couldn't have been fermented. I would have
               thought it was more like fruit juice. Wouldn't
               you, Will?

FATHER: I think it was real wine, Clare. But of course we
               have to bear in mind one very important fact.
               Jesus lived in the Middle East.

MOTHER: I don't quite follow you Will. Surely alcohol is
               evil wherever it's found.

FATHER: It's very different if you live in the Middle East,
               Clair. (With finality) Very different.

Geoffrey asks Dick, the boy down the road, what the Middle East is; and is told it is where people wear hardly any clothes and where they sit on nails.

Geoffrey's religious education is further confused, when his brother John warns him of the terrible danger of worshipping graven images; that could for example even be plasticine models.

Geoffrey is not terribly worried, because he has never been tempted to worship plasticine. At the age of six he is more interested in looking at little girls' willies and has vague qualms of conscience that this might be evil. Furthermore John goes on to point out that Geoffrey is in great danger, because he has used the word 'blimey'. This means he has asked God to blind him. Young Geoffrey tries desperately to say the word backwards, to undo the harm: 'Yemilb! Yemilb!'

However I think he is at his funniest and most poignant when he has to join the youth club, where he first notices girls.

GEOFFREY: I remember that around that time, I'd just read Emily Bronte's 'Wurthering Heights'. I also went to see Laurence Olivier as Heathcliffe and Merle Oberon as Cathy in the film at the local Odeon. What a film that was and what an effect it was to have.

EXCERPT FROM THE FILM'S ORIGINAL SOUND-TRACK: VOICES AND SWEET MUSIC

(LAURENCE OLIVIER as HEATHCLIFFE)

HEATHCLIFFE: Why isn't there the smell of heather in your hair?

(MERLE OBERON as CATHY)

CATHY: Oh, Heathcliffe, why won't you let me come near you? You're not black and horrible as they all think.   You're full of pain. I can make you happy. Let me try. You won't regret it. I'll be your slave. I can bring life back to you.
OLIVIER: Why are your eyes always empty?

TAKE THE FILM SOUND-TRACK BACK BEHIND GEOFFREY'S NARRATION AND GRADUALLY LOSE IT.

GEOFFREY: (NARRATING) Sitting in the front stalls and absorbing all the high drama, an idea occurred to me. Now although I didn't feel I stood a dog's chance of attracting any girls on my own merits, it seemed possible, just possible, that if I could present myself to them as an imitation of Heathcliffe, even as an imitation of Laurence Olivier, I might possibly make some sort of headway. At nights in my bedroom I tried, not very successfully, to imitate his beautiful, carefully delineated voice.

SCENE: GEOFFREY'S BEDROOM

GEOFFREY: (ALOUD) Your hair smells of the heather, Cathy.   No. Your hair! - (BUT HIS VOICE TURNS INTO A SQUAWK)   Your hair - (STILL NOT CONVINCED) Oh blast! (PAUSE) Your hair smells.... that's better. Your hair smells of the heather
(NARRATING) When I tried the Heathcliffe touch with the dumpy little blonde girl at the youth club, the result was slightly embarrassing.

SCENE: YOUTH CLUB

GEOFFREY: (OLIVIER IMITATION) Can I get you a cup of coffee, Mary?
MARY: I don't mind.

GEOFFREY: You like coffee, Mary?

MARY: Are you feeling all right?

GEOFFREY: Feeling all right, Mary?

MARY: Have you got a cold or something?

GEOFFREY: No. Why?

MARY: You sound different.

As director of the play I managed to lay my hands on a few minutes of the original sound-track of the film and so the listener could compare Laurence Olivier's performance and Geoffrey's attempt to model himself on it. Geoffrey Beevers as Geoffrey Parkinson brought a superbly informed naiveté to the role.

During a visit to a production of 'La Boheme', Geoffrey then falls in love with Sybil, another girl from the youth club. He becomes a fervent, if somewhat misinformed, disciple of Freud and begins to drift away from the Chapel. Years later he receives a letter from the minister.

MINISTER: My dear Geoffrey, We have been looking through the list of Church members and notice that you have long since ceased to make a regular attendance. This is a great sadness, not only to us, but also, I am sure, to your dear mother and father. With the greatest reluctance, we have therefore decided that your name must be removed from the membership role. I hope and pray that one day it may be joyfully reinstated. Yours sincerely, Frederick Whitfield Liggett. PS God bless you my boy.

There are two qualities that I particularly love about this play:

1. There are many plays about lapsed faith, in which playwrights tend to attack, or to be embittered by, their childhood faith. They tend neither to offer a positive alternative nor to suggest, that there is more than one side to the question.

2. Very often the reason for writing is a form of personal catharsis and therapy; but, in my opinion, many of these plays do very little to inform, to heal or even to entertain the listener. Geoffrey Parkinson's play is more objective. It

is redeemed by compassion and affection, as well as by acute observation and a lovely sense of humour; that is directed as much at himself as at anybody else. In writing, as in real life, one needs these qualities to get at the truth of a character.

3.   The humour has a slow burn to it. It only occasionally makes us laugh out loud, but it keeps a grin on our faces. It is based on recognition. We may to think to ourselves: 'Oh yes, yes, I know that situation. I have been there and seen that, but I never quite realised before how enlightening and how funny such an everyday situation could be.' As Henry Fielding opines in his preface to *Joseph Andrews*: 'Life everywhere furnishes an accurate observer with the ridiculous.'

Looking At Situation Comedy

The Non-conforming Non-conformist could be said to be a comedy of character. There are some excellent radio comedies, where it is the situation even more than the characters that make us chortle.

One such is *Crisp And Even Brightly* by Alick Rowe (although the characters too are hilarious at times). The play purports to be the true story of Good King Wenceslaus. It won the Sony Comedy Award and ten years later, Miles Kington, one of the judges, still chortled at the memory of it.

This, thematically, was one of a series of plays. The first, *Operation Lightning Pegasus*, purported to be the true story of the siege of Troy and of the wooden horse, which was really the result of a monumental military cock-up by upper class twits on both sides. Achilles was a closet homosexual with a fatal taste in elegant sandals.

The second was called *Odysseus On An Iceberg*. Odysseus was a rotten navigator. He kept taking wrong turns and that's why he landed up on an iceberg and took twenty years to get home. Penelope wasn't worried. She loved having so many suitors.

Both these plays were subsequently given stage performances by many schools. Comedy can be a very effective means of education.

Crisp And Even Brightly points out the many absurdities and anomalies within the Christmas carol of Good King Wenceslaus. I often us the following scene from the play as an exercise when I am working with students on radio acting. It provides an explanation as to how the carol came to be composed.

(SCENE 11. KITCHEN. FX: AN ALARM BELL TOLLS. SMALL CROWD GATHERS.)

LUDMILLA (QUEEN MOTHER):

>Is everybody here and will somebody have that bell silenced? Is everybody here?

(FX: MASSIVE BANGING OF SAUCEPAN WITH SPOON)

CRONE: Quiet. A bit of quiet in my kitchen.

>(SILENCE)
>I should think so.

LUDMILLA: Thank you Crone. Vlad? Good. Otto and Sigmund. Spy? Good. Listen. We have a crisis. Listen. The king is nowhere to be found and there is a page missing.

CRONE: Isn't that just typical.

LUDMILLA: What?

CRONE: Always the same; just when it gets exciting. Just as you get to the best bit of the book. Just when you are get to know -

LUDMILLA: (Over-riding) We are here to discover where he may have gone and what must be done;

remembering of course that security is notoriously lax during the Christmas period and that Slavnik agents are known to be at hand. Speak.

(THIS SECTION SHOULD MOVE VERY FAST)

OTTO: We saw him, Lady, up at his window.

SIGMUND: This evening, early on.

LUDMILLA: What were the conditions?

OTTO: Snow lying, Lady.

SIGMUND: Deep snow.

OTTO: Levelled and honed by the wind and the frost.

SIGMUND: Terrible frost, Lady.

OTTO: Cruel.

LUDMILLA: Suspicious circumstances?

SIGMUND: A poor man, Lady, hanging about.

OTTO: Said he was looking for wood.

SIGMUND: Then the King called down for young Mark. That's his page.

CRONE: Mark the page? Nasty habit.

LUDMILLA: Thank you, Crone.

OTTO: Only the boy was down with us, you see, Lady.

HARRY: That's right. If you remember up he came to the...

THE SPY: ... room, while we were there. After we'd gone the King ordered him to the window and pointed out this so-called-though-now-infinitely-suspicious poor man.

CRONE: Oh, no. 'Peasant' he said he was.

SIGMUND: Who said who said who was?

CRONE: The boy said the King said the poor man was.

VLADIMIR: Certainly, Lady Ludmilla, it was upon the basis that the poor man was a positive peasant that I calculated the relevant provisions.

HARRY: Anyway, the King asked the boy who this poor man or peasant was and where he was from, what sort of house he had.

LUDMILLA: But how do you know all this?

HARRY: Listened through the key hole. That's my job. I'm a spy.

OTTO: The pageboy - he'd be able to give all this information because he'd heard us question the man.

SIGMUND: Yes. Lives just over three miles away.

OTTO: Foot of the forest.

SIGMUND: Just follow the fence.

OTTO: Along to St. Agnes Fountain

EVERYBODY: Where?

LUDMILLA: Anyway.

VLADIMIR: Anyway - flesh, wine and logs were required: pine logs.

CRONE: They were going to deliver it all and be back in time for dinner.

OTTO: Wait a minute -

SIGMUND: The walking woodpile?

OTTO: Right.

SIGMUND: We saw them leave the palace, Lady. Just when the blizzard was starting up.

LUDMILLA: So what we have so far is this:

(THE BREAK-NECK PACE SLOWS DOWN NOW. AS THE NARRATIVE IS TOLD IN THE PALACE, THE MUSIC OF THE CAROL SHOULD CREEP IN BEHIND THE WORDS)

Good King Wenceslas looked out, on the feast of Stephen, when the snow lay round about, deep and crisp and even. Brightly shone the moon that night - though the frost was cruel - when a poor man came in sight, gathering winter fuel.'

CRONE: Fuel?

VLADIMIR: Fuel.

HARRY: 'Hither page and stand by me, if thou knowest its telling: yonder peasant who is he? Where and what his dwelling?'

OTTO: 'Sire he lives a good league hence'

SIGMUND: 'Underneath the mountain Hard against the
                   forest fence'

OTTO: 'By St. Agnes Fountain.'

CRONE: Where?

VLADIMIR: 'Bring me flesh and bring me wine. Bring me
                   pine-logs hither.   Thou and I shall see him
                   dine e'er we dine together.'

OTTO: 'Page -

SIGMUND: 'And Monarch -

OTTO: 'Forth they went;

OTTO/   'Forth they went together
SIGMUND:

ALL: 'Through the rude wind's wild lament

(STOP MUSIC)

LUDMILLA: 'And the bitter weather'. Yes I see. Guards!

OTTO/   Yes, Lady?
SIGMUND:

LUDMILLA: Spy?

HARRY: Yes, Lady?

LUDMILLA: After them. We shall await further reports.
                   (PAUSE) Who was carrying this several
                   hundred-weight of fatuous good will?

OTTO: The boy.

LUDMILLA: As I thought.   And who was leading the way?

SIGMUND: The King.

LUDMILLA: Precisely. They won't have gone far.

Alick Rowe demonstrates an impressive ability to keep the jokes and the invention pouring out page after page, for seventy five minutes. On the day *Crisp And Even Brightly* was broadcast, a friend driving up the M1 told me how many other drivers he had seen, roaring with laughter, and thus he knew who else was listening.

I also still laugh whenever I hear Peter Tinniswood's series of plays about the West Country poacher and philosopher, Winston Heyballs. This excerpt is about whether the middle class family, Winston has adopted, is going to move yet again. It is an inspired and outrageous, politically incorrect diatribe. It is so original, poetic and funny, that he gets way with it, with flying colours.

FATHER   I've decided, Nancy.

NANCY: What have you decided, Father?

FATHER: To move house.

NANCY: Oh my God!

FATHER: It's the wander lust, you see, Old Boy.

NANCY: Wander lust?

FATHER: Yes. Itchy pants.
                 A slow deep yearning in the creaking cockles of
                 the heart.
                 A constant, throbbing ache in the nether
                 regions of the popping crease.

	I want to be off on my travels again, Nancy. I want to experience new sights, new sounds, new smells. I want to be stimulated and excited and enchanted and have my soul completely refurbished.
NANCY:	Father, I'm not going to live in Harrogate again and that is that!
FATHER:	The screech of monkeys and the grunt of tiger. Temple gongs crooning soft in forests thick with teak. Pantiles blistering with summer sun in the Auvergne. The salt spit of winter barges on the Zuider Zee. (PAUSE) Oh my God, I could murder an Eccles cake.
NANCY:	What!?
FATHER:	Well this country's going to the dogs, Nancy. You can't get a decent Eccles cake for love nor money these days. In my youth, in the days of my prime, England was bursting at the seams with Eccles cakes; succulent, sticky, oozing with sensuous spices from the Orient. And then the bloody Nips came along and ruined it all.
NANCY:	What?
FATHER:	The Nips, Old Boy, the Japs. Fearful little slant-eyed stinkers, hell-bent on destroying our planet.

Killing all the dolphins, massacring the whales, poisoning the air we breathe with their ghastly gibbering motor bikes.
What's wrong with Norton and A.G.S and Meschersmitts?
Bloody Nips!
If I had a medium sized tooth pick handy, I'd kebab the whole lot of them, string 'em up as food for the tom tits.
I can't stand Gregorian chant either.

NANCY: What?

FATHER: And Woman's Hour has gone to the dogs too!
Well what do I care about the menstrual problems of one parent lesbian bus conductors?

NANCY: Father, I'm not quite clear what you're getting at.

FATHER: Well, what I'm getting at, Old Boy, is quite simple.
I don't want to live in England any more.

Gillian Reynolds, the courageous and perceptive critic, wrote of *Visiting Julia*, another Peter Tinniswood series: 'There it is, clear as a bell, the individual voice of a writer, who knows his craft, loves his audience, makes brilliant, memorable characters, who unfailingly transform big fears and little failings into laughter.' Dear reader, try and find your own, original voice in this way.

Since his recent death the *Peter Tinniswood Award* has been established by the Society of Authors and the Writers' Guild to perpetuate his memory, as well as to celebrate and encourage high standards in radio drama. There is a yearly play competition.. "The work must be an original piece for radio, and may also include the first episode from an original series or serial." For details see:
www.societyofauthors.net/groups/broadcast/tinniswoodAward.html.

While you are there also have a look at another award for radio playwrights at

www.societyofauthors.net/groups/broadcast/imison.html

7 Writing Short Stories, Dramatisations, Monologues and *The Archers*

Short Story Writing

Writing short stories is simpler - but not necessarily easier - than writing plays and features.

The short story writer will often, in the first half of the story, endeavour to keep the reader in a state of suspended animation. The writer may often only reveal a mood, a mystery, a setting or a character. He may be content to tantalise the reader, knowing that the reader will read on - or even skip forward - to find out what is going to happen. Readers will know, that in the end they should be rewarded with a satisfying twist or resolution.

A classic short story in this genre is *Taste* by Roald Dahl. In the first short paragraph the author sets the scene, a smart dinner party in the sixties. In the second he introduces the famous guest, Richard Pratt, a connoisseur of fine food and wine. The scene is observed by the old family retainer as well as by the reader. Pratt refers to wines as if they were people: 'A rather shy wine, but quite clever.' His wealthy host Mike is in the habit of betting him a case of the wine in question, that he cannot identify it. This evening however Richard appears to be more interested in drooling over Mike's nubile eighteen-year old daughter. So Mike ups the odds. He is a wealthy man and slowly the stake is increased, until he bets Richard anything he likes to name, that he cannot identify the claret. The tension mounts and finally Richard names his price: 'Your daughter in marriage.' Mike accepts: Richard cannot possibly guess such an obscure vineyard. You can imagine Mike's wife's and daughter's reactions. Richard narrows the claret down to a Medoc, to a St. Julien, to the Beychevelle District: 'possibly a Talbot, no - no - a smaller chateau - a Branaire-Ducru' And he's won the nubile daughter!

The story-telling is so compelling, the characterisation so accurate that the reader suspends disbelief. And the twist? The old family retainer has spotted him going into the library, where Mike had left the wine to _chambré_ before dinner. The ending comes as a surprise; but when one thinks about it afterwards, both in terms of situation and of character, it was inevitable. This makes for a powerful and satisfying short story.

Writing For Reading Aloud

I asked my friend the poet, short story writer and playwright, Ted Walker for his view on the difference between a short story read silently and one read aloud. He started by replying, that as a 'Writer of Short Stories for Radio' he was a complete fraud; that he never once sat down to write a story specially for broadcasting. However what he went on to say, demonstrated that as a poet he had been addressing the question of writing to be read aloud for most of his working life.   Ted possesses that endearing combination of qualities, often found in excellent writers: humility and intelligence.

He wrote: 'I think my work may have had some success on air, because I'm a painter _manqué_. When I was a kid, nobody taught me to draw. I grew into manhood terrified, whenever I tried, abysmally, to paint, lest somebody look over my shoulder. I couldn't do it. But then, luckily, my Dad sent me, when I was 10, to learn French with a Monsieur Jupp -- who became Herr Jupp, when we began to play-act in German and Signor Jupp, when, playing the part of a waiter, he started serving invisible pasta. I became a linguist.

I was obsessed, thoroughly entranced, with words; and English words became the best materials for visual communication that I had. The old cliché about 'painting with words' became true for me.

'There's really nothing complicated, I guess, about certain kinds of successful writing for radio. Words _do_ make pictures in the listener's head. (There's a truism for you! But it had better be said yet again, lest the obvious gets lost in theoreticising.) It so happens that my kind of picture-making sometimes works equally well when the words are listened to rather than looked at on the page.

'It must be stressed however that my technique is an intensely *literary* one. I know what I'm up to, while hoping that my reader/listener doesn't. Words don't just *mean* this or that: they *embody* with the sounds they make.

The pictures one creates of an action should catch, with the style of its expression, the very rhythm of what's going on. If you get the rhythm right, the listener or reader, willy-nilly finds himself, -- his limbs, his head, whatever -- joining in. In his imagination he stumbles, or strides out, or hops on one leg. Leslie Norris wrote a poem in which the simple words, 'I wound down the window' occur. Try it aloud: 'I wound down the window'. See? One turn for 'wound' and another for 'down'; the window by now is about three-quarters open, right? And with the arrival of 'window' you've got the glass fully down. The feel of this is all but totally absent from plain old: 'I opened the window.' (Of course, you can't get this effect now that we've got electrically operated windows!)

'Words on the page can be gone over at the reader's leisure, again and again. On radio, you have to get through to the listener *premier coup.* So your story had better not have too complex a narrative thread nor too complicated a plot. A sense of place has to be evoked (the other senses have a vital part to play here: it's not just the eyes that 'see'). Characters must speak -- and (how obvious!) speak *in character*. Possibly more important than *action* is description of what's going on simultaneously with the action. (Smoke coming out of a remote cottage chimney somehow gives more point to the murder that's going on in the kitchen.) Accuracy of detail is vital. You never use words like 'tree' or 'car'; say 'poplar' or 'Rolls'.'

Ted went on to say, 'I think every one of my radio dramas was adapted from one of my *New Yorker* short stories. Again, any success I might have had with radio is down to my particular way of seeing the world. My poetry has the same visual/audio qualities. In a poem in which I remember when my grandfather died, and I had an asthma attack when I was told he was dead, and he had not long since told me that it wasn't yet time to have a bonfire, I had the asthma attack -- alluded to -- actually enacted with the line:

'His fire shot higher than hollyhocks'.

All those aitches, you see, catch the short breaths of asthma.   This is to show how the rabbit is stowed in the top hat. I swear you to secrecy!' Ted has graciously allowed me to lift the veil; so that writer may speak to writer within the pages of this book.

Monologues Are Different

Many of my students at Bath Spa University College and at Bristol University where I teach radio writing modules decide to start by writing monologues, not realising that these and dramatisations are the hardest radio forms to master. A monologue is easier to create on stage, where a character can be seen to move, to interact with props, to dress or undress, to make up, to make telephone calls, etc, etc. Also the space in which she moves is provided and does not have to be evoked. In a radio monologue, as well as telling a story, a character has to create through language and sound effects her appearance, a picture of the space in which operates and any objects she manipulates. This is not easy. It requires the hand of such a master as Peter Tinniswood.

Here is how he does is it in *The Wireless Lady,* specially written for Billie Whitelaw.

The description of the flat is to help the director to create the right acoustic. However notice how with the dialogue alone he both tells the story, while subtly assembling a picture of Winifred. Perhaps she looks a tiny bit like a burrowing animal. Perhaps her feet are slightly too big. She wears glasses. There is something wrong with her leg. Perhaps she has a slight limp. Slowly the listener will begin to fill in these outlines and perhaps to decorate her flat as well. Notice also that sound effects are used very sparingly, but they are used clearly and effectively.

> (THE ACTION TAKES PLACE IN THE DRAWING ROOM OF WINIFRED LESLIE'S FLAT IN HAMPSTEAD. SHE HAS A CAREFULLY REFINED VOICE WHICH LAPSES INTO HER NATIVE NORTHERN WHEN SHE IS EXCITED.

<u>SHE IS AN EXCELLENT ACTRESS AND WHEN</u>
<u>SHE PERFORMS HER EXCERPTS THEY ARE DONE</u>
<u>WITH PANACHE AND FEELING).</u>

WINIFRED: I'm very fond of burrowing animals
I seem to have an affinity with them

(PAUSE)

Many many moons ago I went up for a part in
Coronation Street.
I didn't get it.
They said my feet were too big.
Pity.
It could have been an inroad.

(PAUSE)

I've just had this letter from a producer.
B.B.C.
Wireless.
What he wants is ...
Well, I might as well read it to you.
Let my specs do some work f or a change
instead of loafing around on the end of my
nose.
This is what it says in purple ink: Dear
Winifred Leslie,
",It is a long, time since you appeared on radio.
Scandalously long, if I may be permitted to,
offer humble opinion.
Accordingly I have taken the liberty of writing
to you enclosing a script, which should be
delighted and honoured, if you would consider
performing.
I might add that I have been an ardent admirer
of yours for many years and can say without
fear of contradiction that you are of radio's all
time greats.

I await your reply with eager anticipation.

(PAUSE)

Our milkman's the spitting image "Stinker"
Murdoch.
He used to wear chukka boots.
I wonder what his wife gives him for breakfast.
Nothing I suppose.
Thus is the fate of your average milkman.

(PAUSE)

Chekhov!

I loved acting in the plays of Chekhov on the
wireless.
Mind you, I wasn't one to turn my nose up at
George Formby.
Oh no.
I did three films with George Formby!
Oh yes.
I had the distinction of being the first female
actress ever to ride pillion to George Formby's
motor bike.
He was wearing goggles at the time.
Mean little man he was.
All Brylcream and damp teeth.
"Turned out nice again," he used to say.
I'll say it did.
For him it always turned out nice.
Don't let that gormless grin fool you.
(PAUSE)

I was up all night with my leg.
Do you know what?
I could just fancy a fresh Grapefruit

(FX: RUSTLE OF THE LETTER)

> This producer chappie - I can't read his name
> you know.

Writing Dramatisations

The classic serial remains one of the BBC's most successful and long-standing slots and the art of dramatising novels is alive and well. The BBC will only invite experienced playwrights to undertake the task, as experience of how radio drama works and engages the listener is essential. If you do decide to go ahead, you should check with the publisher that the copyright in the novel is available. The author or his estate retain the copyright for 75 years after the death of the author of the date of publication, whichever is later.

It is often necessary to take considerable liberties with the structure of a novel, in order to convey the essence of the work to the listener in an engaging and compelling manner. The experience of reading, where one can close or open a book or go back or skim forward, is very different from that of listening to the continuum of a radio play. Dramatists cannot afford to be as discursive as novelists. Also the beginning of a dramatisation is crucial. While one can read oneself slowly into a novel, this cannot be the case with a dramatisation.

One of the first English novels, *Joseph Andrews* by Henry Fielding, begins: 'It is a trite but true observation, that examples work more forcibly on the mind than precepts: and if this be just in what is odious and blameable, it is more strongly so in what is amiable and praiseworthy.' It is assumed by the author, that the reader has all the time in the world to share his reflections, before getting caught up in the story. The dramatisation on the other hand needs either to project the listener into an involving story or at least to entertain him from the outset.

In his dramatisation of *Joseph Andrews*, John Scotney decided to give us some of Fielding's more entertaining philosophising on the subject of chastity; before plunging us into the story.

This also allowed us to participate in the authorial voice, an important element in this novel, and to gain something of the flavour of the period. Here is the beginning:

> (TECHNICAL NOTE: THE PRODUCTION SHOULD
> BE SEAMLESS. THEREFORE THE SCENES SIMPLY
> INDICATE POSSIBLE RECORDING BREAKS.
> OFTEN FX AND BACKGROUND FROM A
> PREVIOUS SCENE WILL TUCK UNDER SPEECH
> FROM A FOLLOWING SCENE)

ANNOUNCER: 'Joseph Andrews' by Henry Fielding, dramatised in four episodes by John Scotney.

> (MUSIC: A LIVELY AND HUMOROUS
> EIGHTEENTH CENTURY PASTICHE)

FIELDING (as NARRATOR):
The first part, which treats of the death of Sir Thomas Booby, with the affectionate and mournful behaviour of his widow and the great chastity of Joseph.

ACTRESS 1: (Fervently respectful) Chastity!

ACTRESS 2: (Ditto) Chastity!

PARSON: (Ditto) Ah yes, chastity!
ADMAS

> (SEVERAL OTHER LADIES WITH…)

LADY BOOBY: (Mocking) What!

FIELDING: Nay, is not male chastity as becoming to the human species as female? Yet the character of a chaste man is a thing few authors among the moderns have seen fit to dwell upon.

ACTRESS 1:	Whilst female chastity is everywhere to be found, at least in the book shops.
ACTRESS 2:	(<u>Catty</u>) Who has not heard of the celebrated chastity of sweet, dear, pretty Pamela Andrews?
ACTOR:	So admirably recorded by Mr. Samuel Richardson in his 'Pamela'.

ACTRESS 2: (<u>Over-sweetly</u>) Or - Virtue Rewarded.'

<u>(NEXT FEW SPEECHES ARE HYPOCRITICALLY PRURIENT</u>)

ACTRESS 1:	Pamela, a pretty fifteen-year old, servant girl, artlessly sets down how she virtuously resisted all manner of lewd and lustful assaults by her master - including an attempted rape,
ACTOR 2:	Which she describes in some detail.
ACTRESS 1:	Until defeated at last by her chastity, her master offered her the joy of becoming his wife.
ACTRESS 2:	And so was able legitimately to enjoy those attentions,

<u>(LADIES BEGIN TO LAUGH</u>)

	he had so often attempted to enforce on her in vain.
ACTOR 1:	Such a theme is the soul of religion, good breeding (<u>UNCTUOUS</u>) and morality in our present age; and the pulpit as well as the coffee house has resounded with Pamela's praise.
ACTOR 2:	But what of her brother?

JOSEPH: Mr. <u>Joseph</u> Andrews, who by keeping his
                  sister's virtues ever before his eyes,

ADAMS: and attending to the wise advice of the
                  Reverend Mr. Abraham Adams

JOSEPH: was also able to preserve <u>his</u> chastity in the face
                  of as many and as great temptations as were
                  placed before his sister.

ACTRESS 1: Who has heard of him?

               <u>(MUSIC OUT, RATHER SHARPLY,)</u>

ACTRESS 2:   Who among those thousands to whom the
                  name '<u>Pamela</u> Andrews' is now so familiar, has
                  heard of <u>Joseph</u> Andrews?

ACTOR 1:   To correct the which omission we now present
                  before the public the authentic:

               <u>(A COMIC CHORD OR TWO OF MUSIC)</u>

FIELDING: *History of the Adventures of Joseph Andrews and
                  his friend, Mr. Abraham Adams,* as faithfully
                  recorded by your servant, Mr Henry Fielding,
                  Gent.

               <u>(UNDER THE END OF PREVIOUS SPEECH
               ESTABLISH THE JOYFUL PEELING OF ENGLISH
               CHURCH BELLS AND RUSTICS MURMURING
               'YOUR HONOUR')</u>

FIELDING :   Our history opens in the year of Grace, 1737,
                  upon a Sunday morning in summer

(ADD BIRDSONG)

> as Parson Adams walks through the
> churchyard, receiving the bows and salutations
> of his flock -

And so the play has started and the story proper may now begin.
Several points have been established in this opening passage:

1. John Scotney was able to introduce the full title and thus
   something of the eighteenth century flavour of the novel
   without its seeming longeur.

2. We are informed that the novel was intended as a satire
   upon the recently published, 'first' English novel, *Pamela*
   by Samuel Richardson.

3. The author, Henry Fielding, will be the narrator.

4. However he will share this function with his main
   characters, who will often introduce and describe
   themselves, as do Joseph and Adams and a voice we may
   later recognise as Lady Booby's. This convention seemed
   very much to belong to Fielding's style of making asides.

5. The opening scene has been introduced.

There is not space here to take you through this dramatisation of
Joseph Andrews step by step. However let me give you some
general pointers. Apart from accomplishing the vitally important
opening, the dramatiser will need to compile a thorough synopsis
of the plot. He can then break the novel down into episodes.
Classic serial episodes are normally about 57 minutes long and
there are also usually some slots for modern novels dramatised in
27 minute episodes.

Compelling 'cliff-hangers' will help persuade the listeners to
make a date with future episodes. However the dramatiser should
not assume that the listener will have heard previous episodes and
thus from the second episode on 'action so far' should be

economically and entertainingly included in the beginning of each episode.

Finally the writer should then break each episode down into variety of scenes to keep the listener as enthralled as possible.

Strangely enough the next section on *The Archers* might also give some help in this respect.

Scriptwriting For *The Archers*

I am firmly of the opinion that there is only room for one soap opera on national radio. The BBC has had a spate of managers, who have asked drama producers, 'Where are the *Eastenders,* the *Bills,* the *Casualtys* of radio?' These managers have mostly come from television and have not fully grasped, how differently radio works. It can take a dedicated listener several years to identify with the characters in a radio soap opera, to create the settings in their imaginations, to feel that an 'Ambridge' is part of their daily lives.

The Archers, the world's longest running soap opera, is now in its fifty third year. It had already made a national impact in 1955 when Grace Archer was burnt to death trying to rescue a horse from a blazing stable. This was a highly successful audience-stealing ploy on the night that ITV was launched.

Now under the editorship of Vanessa Whitburn it enjoys an audience on Radio 4, digital radio and over the Internet of almost 5,000,000; with a popular *Archers Addicts* fan club. See www .archers-addicts.com.

There is a basic team of ten writers, who with the guidance of the Editor and the producers, keep the stories flowing year after year.

Should you want to become one of these writers, you should send off to The Mailbox, Birmingham B1 1RF for 'The Archers Pack.' Following the brief therein, you can then write an episode on spec. If you surmount this hurdle and are considered promising, you will be invited to a mock script conference. After this you will be sent away to write a synopsis for a week's storylines. 'This is the real killer' says Caroline Harrington, one of the writing team. Each week there are six episodes of twelve and a half minutes each and each episode should have an average of five scenes. Each episode should have about seven characters and the continuities of the major (three month stories) and minor stories (of about a month) need to be kept going.

One of your problems is that, unlike TV soap opera, characters rarely leave. Thus death and divorce can very rarely be part of the plot-lines. Listen for yourself and note down, what the major and minor stories are, running through each episode over a week or more.

On the other hand unlike the TV soaps, *The Archers* don't have any actors on regular contract. Thus the writers cannot guarantee that they will necessarily have the cast they ideally want with which to carry a story. Hence when the Editor is asked what qualities she looks for in a prospective Archers writer, she replies, "a talent for juggling."

When writer Louise Page was on the team, Vanessa Whitburn has fond memories of asking her to carry a comedy story in which Jean Paul, the precious chef at Grey Gables, accidentally poisoned some guests by feeding them toadstools. They had been swapped for mushrooms by one of the Grundy kids. The only problem was could Louise Page write the story without Jean Paul!? In fact she did a great job, majoring on Ed Grundy and his Mum Clarrie and carrying a lot in gossip with Lynda Snell   "That's the kind of flexibility you need on The Archers team", says Vanessa.

She continues "You also need to be fast and accurate and not panic. When Foot and Mouth hit out of the blue we were in studio and recording scenes that we knew would not work on transmission. The writers were called in and changed scenes on the spot to keep up with the breaking news. Thereafter we split the team into two for about 6 months whilst the crisis ravaged the countryside. One team worked on the continuing drama whilst the other team filled in a continuing story concerning Foot and Mouth and how it impacted on Ambridge."

Incidentally there is an interesting problem for dramatists with modern farming as most of it is a lonely process and lengthy internal monologues on tractors are not exactly *The Archers* style.

On the contrary The Archers has developed an engaging style that attracts a massive audience. Also its cunning afternoon scheduling, before the single play, helps to build an audience for radio drama in general.

As long as you do not lose your original voice or vision, your vocation, writing for *The Archers* can be a very good training for other forms of radio writing.

International Soap

Just as *the Archers* was instituted under the guise of entertainment to relay information to farmers and help with our agricultural recovery after World War II, so the BBC World Service Trust is promoting radio soap operas to help solve economic and social problems in Russia (in which Tony Blair made a guest appearance as himself), Romania, Albania, Afghanistan and Myanmar and are planning ones in Vietnam and in Southern Iraq. Other organisations such as *Health Unlimited* in Cambodia and Somaliland and the American *PCI* (*Population Communications International*) in Tanzania, Kenya and India are also helping to promote family health, stable communities and sustainable environment and to combat the spread of HIV/AIDS through radio soap opera. The formula of 90% entertainment and 10% information and message has proved most effective in influencing listeners' hearts, minds and actions. I would recommend all radio playwrights to bear this in mind.

The BBC World Service also has its own English soap with the largest radio drama audience in the world. If you are a night owl listen to *Westway* and if you want to write for it, approach one of the producers. You can listen to recent episodes online at:

http://www.bbc.co.uk/worldservice/arts/features/westway/index.shtml

8 Writing and Compiling a Radio Feature

Defining A Radio Feature

The earliest radio drama with a few exceptions consisted of stage plays, adapted for radio. Before the war in Manchester and Bristol, G.D. Bridson and Francis Dillon were experimenting with unscripted recordings of local speech to make pure radio features. In 1945 the Features Department moved to London, where producers experimented with the medium to create works of art specially written for radio. Such were Dylan Thomas' *Under Milkwood* and Louis MacNeice's *The Dark Tower*. However by the 1960's most new ideas and scripts submitted to BBC Radio were specifically written for radio in the first place.

Today the term feature has come to mean anything from a five minute report on the chicken industry, recorded on location, to an open ended Dominican Debate on the Existence of God on Radio 3. For the purpose of this chapter I shall take it to mean a creative piece of writing and production, where the elements do not consist solely of scripted drama as we traditionally understand them. Very often as in the form called 'Drama Documentary' or 'Faction' they will be constructed out of fact, rather than out of fiction.

As in previous chapters, I can best illustrate this from my own productions, not because they are better than others, but simply because I know the intentions, that inform them and how they were put together.

One of my happier and more productive working relationships in the field of features has been with the writer, Mike Walker. He is prolific of ideas and of fresh approaches and I have tried in turn to be his guide, philosopher and friend; to help him realise what I think will work splendidly and to modify and clarify, what might be confusing or alienating to the listener. As I shall explain in the next chapter I think the producer has as much as possible to put himself in the place of the listener.

One of our first joint ventures was a feature about Chief Sitting Bull of the Sioux Indians, called *A Warrior I Have Been*. Mike was particularly interested in exploring the differing mindset and cultural values of the Red Indians and of the White Americans in the 19th century. He pointed out to me how much more formal and prepared was the speech of the Indians. He suggested that their lines should be scripted, in the form of blank verse, containing a measured authority. They would have a sense of the importance of the spoken word, the holiness of the oral tradition, common to mankind before the invention of printing and of the media. They might speak in the considered way, that one has to, when speaking through an interpreter. To contrast with this he suggested, that to the actors portraying White soldiers, we should give fact sheets, upon which they should improvise. If they stumbled, searched for words and were garbled in their delivery, this would be appropriate. Not only were many of them not very well educated, but perhaps in their heart of hearts they were uneasy at their treatment of the Indians and this unease might betray itself in incoherence.

The listener would not know that we had prepared the feature in this way, but if we had got it right the result, the production would ring true.

Here are two examples of what I mean. The first is a transcript of a White official:

> My name's Macloughlin, Injun agent at Standin' Rock. Now, I reckon I'm a reasonable man, but (Sighs) I just cánt understand why Sitting Bull won't tow the godamned line just like most of the other Injuns on the reservation. I mean, well let's face it now the days of the Injun are over. When Sitting Bull surrendered came back from Canada that was it. Trouble is our Sitting Bull isn't like those Injuns who co-operated or let me set 'em up as chiefs or members of the Injun police. Not on your life. When there's trouble you can bet he's in on it'.

How different is the prepared and measured language of one of the Indians:

Listen.

I, Wanbli Sapa, Black Eagle, was there.

It was before dawn.

Sitting Bull, Tatanka Yotanka, was sleeping in his cabin.

The door was kicked open and the police came in.

They said, they'd come to arrest him.

They said, that they were holding him.

They said, that if he resisted them, he would be killed where he was.

He said, 'Yes.'

He had to dress and they helped him, trying to be quick before any others should come and interrupt their work.

They were clumsy.

They pushed him through the door.

He was not properly dressed.

His dignity was hurt to be seen by the people in this way.

But he was not afraid.

The police were afraid.'

Notice how many pictures are created by the Indian's speech. The agent's speech on the other hand conveys mainly his subjective emotions.

Australia

Still on the subject of one culture clashing with another, Mike Walker was pretty shrewd in 1979. He asked me whether I knew that 1988 would be the bicentenary of the first white settlement of Australia. He outlined a possible Drama Documentary series of thirteen one hour programmes, taking us from the first records of Aborigine culture up to the bicentenary ceremonies in 1988. We came to christen the series 'The Long March of Every Oz'.

Thirteen hours may seem ample, but when you have the entire history of a nation to cover, it can seem limiting. Mike suggested that we should paint a rich historical tapestry of activities and events with a contemporary commentator as guide. Thus an Australian version of a Michael Palin or Alan Whicker as a time traveller, strolling through the action, would point out the convicts building the first settlement, the early gold diggers in Melbourne buying their provisions and their whores or a Victorian lady settler in the outback playing an upright piano just imported from Liverpool.

Against this background we should have comment from some of Australia's leading historians of contrasting political persuasions and we should have readings from source material such as journals, letters home, transcripts of trials, bills of lading, etc.

Then with careful multi-tracking and sound balance, so that we did not confuse the listener with too much complexity of sound, we should weave in and out of a background of work songs, military orders, drunken brawls, cattle herding, copper mining, etc, etc.   Most of our backgrounds were recorded on location, while our foregrounds were recorded mostly in the studio.

This was the basic technique, though with many variations and with telling quieter sequences. It required much time spent in post production.

The earlier episodes were recorded almost entirely in the U.K and the later ones in Australia. The break point between the two was made by a fairly arbitrary decision on our part as to when, where and how the Australian accent evolved from an amalgam of British and Irish accents. Some joke that it started, because the Australians kept their mouths half closed, so the flies wouldn't get in. Try speaking that way and you should see what I mean. Others say the upward inflexion at the end of a sentence is due to their coming from a government run country, where people are naturally deferential.

However several historians suggested, that the accent developed from such bush rangers, outlaws and outback 'boyos' as Ned Kelly in the 1880's. Young rebels, in this case the poor Irish versus the English settlers, might well have developed their own slang and intonation as a badge of identity. We settled for this last theory. It made a nice breakpoint in the in the historical, dramatic narrative.

Another challenging problem in such a series is that of mixing sources, which are read by actors, with excerpts from recorded interviews. Actors by contrast will often sound 'performed' and the interviewees more real. To overcome this we often adopted a similar technique, to that which we used for the White Americans in *A Warrior I Have Been*. We gave fact sheets or resumés to the actors and asked them to rephrase them in their own words.

I should like to take you through some of the last episode of the series, to demonstrate how we attempted to overcome some of the problems we encountered. The episode consisted mostly, but no means entirely of 'vox-pop'. It was entitled *Lucky Country?* The irony of the question mark was intended.

Handling 'Vox-Pop' In Features

We wanted to contrast the poet's view of the quiet, timeless life of the bush with the business of the urban, twentieth century; so we started with *Noonday Axeman* by Les Murray, Australia's leading contemporary poet:

<u>BIRDS, CRICKETS, ETC: THE MUTED SOUNDS OF THE AUSTRALIAN BUSH AT MIDDAY.</u>

ACTOR: Axe-fall, echo and silence. Noonday silence.
Two miles from here, it is the twentieth century: cars on the bitumen, power lines vaulting the farms.
Here, with my axe, I am chopping into the stillness.
Axe-fall, echo and silence. I pause, roll tobacco, twist a cigarette, lick it. All is still.

<u>INTRODUCE PEACEFUL MUSIC</u>

I lean on my axe. A crowd of fragrant leaves hangs over me, moveless, pierced everywhere by sky.

The poem continues and the peaceful music segues into the title music.

We talked long and hard about whether we should have the sound of the axe chopping into the wood. We finally decided against it. It is there in the poem. Radio is about providing an outline, that the listener can fill in. As well as pictures the listeners can imagine sounds, smells and the feeling of things. Things can be all the more perfect, all the more powerful and evocative for being imagined. Let us not interrupt the listener doing her work.

The bespoke music, however, composed by Elizabeth Parker, is introduced at the precise moment that it can most effectively intensify and prolong the pictures already forming in our mind.

May I suggest that as an exercise you attempt to analyse the different elements - scripted readings, interviews, actuality etc - that we had to record and assemble in this opening and in the following (abrid excerpt. See if it tallies with the list I shall give at the end of the passage.

EPIC THEME MUSIC IS FADED DOWN

ANNOUNCER: Episode Thirteen: 'Lucky Country? ?' After the boom, multiculturalism and the search for new values.

SWELL MUSIC AND THEN FADE TO SILENCE
MANNING-CLARKE (Historian):

I was very enthusiastic about Gough Whitlam, because he was one of those gifted men, who believed the labour movement could create a society, in which there was equality of opportunity, without spiritual popery, without conformism and without pandering to mediocrity.

START SONG: 'TIME FOR FREEDOM' IN BACKGROUND. WEAVE IN AND OUT OF FOLLOWING SPEAKERS

WOMAN: I don't think deep down we actually believed it could happen.

MAN 1:   A lot of people clearly felt it was time.

MAN 2:   We had years and years of conservative government under Menzies and he tried to do things for Australia in a hurry.   He knew that the forces of reaction would get him out of power.

MAN 3:   We were in a period of decline, brought about by the skilful manipulative moves of the new president of the trade union movement of Australia, Mr. Robert James Lee Hawke. Inflation was on the rise.   Unemployment was rising.   Liberals were hoisted and Gough's banner 'it's time' was all the go

SWELL SONG 'TIME FOR FREEDOM' TO CONCLUSION AND MIX WITH ACTUALITY OF GOUGH WHITLAM'S SPEECH. USE THE CROWD'S SPONTANEOUS CHEERS TO WEAVE IN AND OUT OF HIS SPEECH AND OF VOX POP

WHITLAM: Men and women of Australia, there are moments in history when the whole fate and future of nations can be decided by a single decision. For Australia this is such a time.

CHEERS

MAN 4:   I was a fan of Whitlam.   Whitlam embodied many of things that Menzies had, funnily enough, this tall, leonine, silver-haired figure with fluent tongue and persuasive arguments. I suppose, people wanted to revere him in a similar fashion

CHEERS

WHITLAM: We will abolish conscription forthwith.

CHEERS

NARRATOR: During their first few days in office labour
                  made sweeping changes.

WHITLAM: Not just because a volunteer army is a better
                  army, but because it's intolerable that a free
                  nation at peace and not under threat should cull
                  by lottery the best of its youth to provide
                  defence on the cheap.

CHEERS

HUMPHREY MACQUEEN (Marxist Historian)
                  These were people who believed that there was
                  enough wealth in the country to do something
                  for the poor and for Aborigines and that it was
                  no longer necessary to despoil the environment
                  in order to have enough dirt to sell to the
                  Japanese.

WHITLAM: We will legislate to give the Aborigines land
                  rights.

CHEERS

MACQUEEN: Questions like Urban planning and the
                  environment and the Arts entered into the
                  political agenda.

WHITLAM: Australians are diminished while the
                  Aborigines are denied their rightful place in
                  this nation.

CHEERS

WOMAN 2:   The two most important things that happened
             early in the Whitlam period were freedom of
             education and withdrawal of troops from
             Vietnam.

WHITLAM: It's time for a new team, a new programme, a
             new drive for equality of opportunities. Time
             for a new vision of what we achieve in this
             generation for our nation.

CHEERS

MAN 5:   The Labour Government spent like drunken
             sailors. Government spending increased by
             seventy five percent. Wages exploded by over
             fifty percent.

MAN 6:   Prices went through the roof. When you think
             ten dollars and somebody comes along and
             says 'think a hundred', the whole spectrum of
             the community changes.

MAN 5:   Businesses went to the wall.

MACQUEEN: The people who attacked him were saying,
             'there's too much governmental activity of
             every kind in every way.'

WHITLAM: We ought to be angry with a deep determined
             anger that a country as rich and skilled as ours
             should be producing so much inequality, so
             much poverty so much that is shoddy and sub-
             standard. We ought to be angry with an
             unrelenting anger that our Aborigines have the
             world's highest infant mortality rate.

CLAPPING

We ought to be angry on our children's behalf, at the mindless destruction of our national and historical heritage.

CHEERS

MACQUEEN: Australian intellectual life really came of age since the seventies with Patrick White's winning of the Nobel Prize, with Australians winning the Booker Prize, with the Australian film industry.

NARRATOR: McDonald's opened their first take-away, wine boxes appeared, the Sydney Opera House was opened.

BLASTS AND WHOOPS OF SHIPS' SIRENS IN SIDNEY HARBOUR, VAST CROWD CHEEERING, ACTUALITY FROM THE DAY OF THE OPENING.

GIRL: The Queen came to open it. It was really exciting. Everyone loved it. It was exciting for us and she came and did a tour. And all the schools were out in force and waved and she waved back - at me!

NARRATOR: It was a boom time, enhanced by the richness of the nations mineral reserves. Nothing seemed impossible.

MACQUEEN: We could buy champagne and caviar till the cows came home and this kept to push up the value of the dollar until by 1974 the Australian dollar was worth 1.44 American dollars. We were on the crest of the wave. We could travel around the world, everything was cheap.   It was the bonanza years of selling off Australia.

SONG 'LADY SUNSHINE'

MAN 9:	Well if it's good enough for Whitlam it's good enough for me, because it's the first decent, bloody government we've ever had for twenty three years.

SWELL SONG AGAIN: 'LADY SUNSHINE, LET YOUR SUN SHINE ON ME'

I have quoted at length, because I should like to invite you to think not only about how this first twenty minutes of *'Lucky Country? ?'* works for the listener, but to examine how it was put together.

Examining The Building Blocks Of A Feature

Assembling the foregoing was a complex and time-consuming process. Let's look at the different elements – or building blocks - that go to make up the whole.

1. There was the scripted reading of the poem by an actor recorded in a BBC studio in Bristol, England.

2. Epic title music to give us the sense of scale of such a large island nation and of the sweep of history. The listener, hopefully, will have come to identify with this music over the past twelve episodes.

3. There was the woman announcer, recorded in an ABC Studio in Sidney, who gives us the title and the theme of the episode. (The credits are left to the end).

4. Interviews with two leading historians were recorded in a studio in Canberra. Mike Walker prepared a series of questions for them, which we asked them to respond to as spontaneously, coherently and concisely as they could. One of the problems of putting together a feature of this nature is the amount of repetition and meandering, that one has to edit out. If you can brief the interviewee effectively and train him to contain your question within his answer, you can save hours of editing.

5. Vox-pop interviews edited to advance the story, to represent both sides of the political equation and to convey the excitement and hope at the election of Gough Whitlam in 1975. Probably the most strenuous part of the exercise were the days and days of gathering and then editing down to identifiable, meaningful and attractive sound-bites: literally hundreds of hours of interviews with ordinary Australians.

6. Other interviews were kindly provided from the archives of the Australian Broadcasting Company, as was the recording of Gough Whitlam's speech and as were the recordings of crowds and ships sirens from the opening of the Sidney Opera House.

7. Under the BBC's agreement with the Performing Rights Society we were able to use the songs 'It's Time' and 'Mr. Sunshine'.

8. Wild track recordings (for dramatic license and technical interweaving) of crowds cheering and responding. As much as possible we used the authentic and actual responses to Whitlam's speech. Dramatically it was important, that these sounded spontaneous and heartfelt and that they conveyed the appropriate celebration and exuberance. Also there were background recordings of birdsong, etc from the BBC's and the ABC' recorded sound effects libraries.

9. Rather late in this episode we introduce the narrator to link speakers and to convey some necessary information. Some listeners may recognise him as our guide from previous episodes. Others may think he is just another vox pop interviewee. It does not matter. The same may be true of Humphrey MacQueen, the second historian.

So this was the raw material as it were. How did we plan the operation? Then how did we assemble and put together the material?

In the first place, Mike Walker produced a draft outline of our intentions and objectives and of the proposed structure of the programme. In this final episode, we knew that we wanted to convey as broad a spectrum of every aspect of Australian life and attitudes as possible from the accession of Whitlam in 1972 to the bicentenary in 1988.

We planned to use Les Murray's poem, *Noonday Axeman* to open and close the programme and to link one part to another. We planned to convey the rise of Whitlam and the story of Cyclone Tracey in the first part; the sacking of Whitlam by Her Majesty's Governor General and a canter through descriptions of Australia's mineral resources, multiculturalism, religion, sport and crime in the second part; and to have the bicentennial celebrations and reflections on the possible future of Australia in the final part.

That was the blueprint or foundation. The building might be very different. Much of the creative work was done in post-production at our Bristol studio, where as producer I consulted Mike Walker and Andrew Lawrence, the chief BBC technician over the final mix.

We have spent a long time on this particular programme, but I should like to take you through a few more edited highlights, to demonstrate some more possible elements and ways of assembling them. With less and less costly and more efficient digital editing software, we are entering the age of a person director/author/editor and this may be the way you, the reader/writer/director, may like to work in the future. A little later in the programme:

INTRODUCE QUIET SLIGHTLY OMINOUS MUSIC

MAN: We were all brainwashed. The Messiah had offered us the world, but three years down the track we realised he was just a politician.

MANNING: He was a charismatic personality, but he
-CLARKE was in the great river of life...

THE MUSIC COMPLEMENTS THE THEME.

... Things went wrong - Partly because Gough was not a very good judge of other men and he made some tragic mistakes in the choice of people to work with.

WOMAN: His fatal flaw was to try to do too much too soon.

MAN: The fear of change began to seep darkly into the bottoms of the bellies of all of us.

NARRATOR: Nature so often a force in Australian life chose to exhibit its power in 1974 when the city of Darwin was struck by Cyclone Tracey.

LOSE MUSIC. THREE SECONDS SILENCE (THE CALM BEFORE THE STORM)

WOMAN 2:   We had two small earth tremors and the mangoes ripened very early and all the ants were in frenetic activity. Well, the Aborigines know their signs and in the two weeks before Cyclone Tracey some of the old Aborigines just rolled up their swags and left.

ACTUALITY NEWS BROADCAST (HISSY QUALITY):

NEWSCASTER: And here's the latest cyclone warning. At three Cyclone Tracey was centred 80 kilometres north west of Darwin and moving south easterly at seven kilometres per hour.

MIX OF THOUSANDS OF FROGS CROAKING WITH RADIOPHONIC MUSIC

WOMAN 2:   And then the frogs started. And Illiwara the old Aborigine said, 'If the frogs sing out very loud, well then look out'. They started off in a

slow chorus and then by the time dusk fell it
was a screaming frenzy.

HEIGHTEN MUSIC AND FROG EFFECTS

WOMAN 3:   (SHOUTING ABOVE THE DIN) We came
home about six o'clock. We had to fill
everything we had with water, lock the
windows, seal the doors.

LOSE FROGS AND MUSIC. INTRODUCE SLIGHT WIND

WOMAN 2:   You heard a distant moaning and then it got
louder and louder. I was going to put my
daughter in the land rover and make a run for
it, but my husband said just look out there and
clumps of trees were rushing past the house
and some people did try to make a run for it
and were killed.

STEEPLY INCREASE NOISE OF BUFFETING WIND

WOMAN 4:   Ours was a tropical house with louvres. The
wind could get out. In houses where it couldn't
get out, they just exploded with the pressure.

WOMAN 5:   There was a great tree at the back of our house
and in that tree there was a refrigerator.

INTERVIEWER: You were under the bed with your Mummy?

SMALL GIRL: Yeah, it was terrible.

MIX WIND INTO 'AFTERMATH' MUSIC

WOMAN 2:   When the daylight came we looked out on a
scene of utter desolation. Where trees and

	houses had been there were just stumps and rubble.
MAN:	I saw a boat half way up a hill.

After a few more speeches describing the aftermath:

<u>LOSE MUSIC</u>

EMERGENCY BROADCAST (FROM THE TIME):	
	"…people of Darwin, this is General Alan Stretton, the civilian chief of the natural disasters organisation"
WOMAN 4:	The looting was indescribable. To me it was like something out of a movie. My daughter was bending over looking at this wedding photograph and well a man made an obvious movement...
	I won't go into that, it's too awful and I saw that they were rapists, so I raced and got the gun and I said, 'I'll kill you' and they knew I meant it and they took off.
EMERGENCY BROADCAST:	
	"We must stop rumours. There are rumours about the police shooting people, when in fact it was Tiger Brennan probably shooting the dogs."
WOMAN 3:	And nature reasserted itself. (<u>Giggles</u>) There were people making love all over the place. I passed a house of which there was nothing left except the floorboards and one double bed. It was like Salvador Dali. And there were two people in bed making love, quite oblivious to who might be going past and it didn't matter. (LAUGHS)

<u>BIRDSONG AND CRICKETS AS AT BEGINNING OF
PROGRAMME. HOLD FOR SEVERAL SECONDS.</u>

ACTOR: After the tree falls, there will reign the same
                         silence as stuns and spurs us, enraptures and
                         defeats us, as seems to some a challenge and
                         seems to others to be waiting here for
                         something beyond imagining.

Thus we told the story of Cyclone Tracey, through carefully
selected and edited vox pop interviews and through radio
broadcasts from the time. We orchestrated or counterpointed the
atmosphere with sound effects and with radiophonic music.

I should like to share one final element, that we used in this
episode: a swearing in ceremony, in which new citizens are taking
the oath of allegiance. Recording it was a moving experience.

<u>ACOUSTIC OF LARGE HALL. QUIET
BACKGROUND CHAT AND SINGING,
PARTICULARLY OF SMALL CHILDREN, IN
MANY LANGUAGES</u>

SWEARING IN OFFICER:

                         In a few minutes you will be all equal
                         Australian citizens. At the ceremony we have
                         people here from Yugoslavia, Libya, South
                         Africa, Afghanistan, New Zealand, Turkey,
                         United Kingdom, Vietnam, Chile, Hong Kong,
                         France, Argentina, Portugal, Ireland, Canada,
                         Finland, Pakistan, Indonesia, Philippines,
                         Korea, Malaysia, Spain, Sri Lanka, Greece,
                         Lebanon and Taiwan. (<u>FOLDS PAPER</u>) And
                         that spells multi-culturalism to me. I'm sure it
                         does to you too.

Illustrating A First Person Feature

I should also like to share with you a more personal feature, that I made in the eighties. It is the kind of feature that you as writer, sound recordist, producer and editor could put together yourself.

I had attended a lecture by a University tutor, who with his fifteen-year old son, had cycled through France and Spain along the ancient pilgrimage route to Santiago de Compostella in Galicia. I had saved up some leave and was inspired to do the same with my then twelve year old son, Seamus. We planned to cut costs, in the five weeks it would take to cycle the 1,100 miles by taking a tent. At that time, I had in Robin Hicks the most enlightened BBC boss. He was a true enabler and encourager. He said, 'don't take a tent. That would be like carrying England on your back'. Instead he urged me to take a tape recorder and offered to cover the modest expenses of two poor pilgrims. Furthermore he funded the buying of one of our two new bikes. At the time he was criticised by other BBC managers for profligacy; but the programme came out well under budget and was so popular, that it was broadcast four times.

The shape of the programme was simple. It was that of pilgrims, throughout the ages, making the pilgrimage. Seamus and I were simply the most recent among the multitudes, who had gone that way before.

Here are the first five minutes. May I suggest you count the elements: scripted speech, actuality, pre-recorded music, etc, and think about how you would plan the shape, and record and assemble these elements. I will explain at the end of the passage.

ANNOUNCER: A reflective pilgrim on the road to Santiago always makes a double journey: The backward journey through time and the forward journey through space.

(INTRODUCE MEDIAEVAL HARP MUSIC BY MARY REMNANT)

Every step the pilgrim makes evokes memories of those who passed that way ever since the discovery of the tomb of the Apostle James in the Ninth Century.

READER: *(FROM JACQUES DE VORAGINES)* When St. James was beheaded, his disciples placed his body in a boat without a rudder and an angel of the Lord guided them to Galicia, the Kingdom of Queen Lupa.
When the disciples asked her for a burial place she set them a series of trials. In the last of these they were attacked by two wild bulls. They made the sign of the cross over them and the bulls became as gentle as lambs.
The disciples followed a star, until it stopped. There they buried St. James. This was in a field called *the field of the star*, or Compostela.

ANNOUNCER: The Field of the Star. Last year Shaun MacLoughlin was among the five or six hundred pilgrims who walked, cycled or rode horseback to Santiago de Compostela in Spain. His companion was his son, Seamus.

(FADE MUSIC)

SEAMUS: My dad told me we were going to cycle to Santiago. He just told me, but now I'm glad I went. It was about 1,100 miles and took us around five and a half weeks. I was 12 then, but now I'm 13 and we both kept diaries.

(ACTUALITY RECORDING OF DEPARTURE)

MOTHER: Just be careful. Right?

SEAMUS: (TO SMALL SISTER) Binnie, get off my - Don't put your foot in the pedal, Binnie. The whole thing will tip over.

MOTHER: Right? Right? And just be careful.

SEAMUS: Yeah.

MOTHER: Won't you?

(<u>LOSE ACTUALITY</u>)

SEAMUS: At 3.29 pm we set off for Temple Meads, and I recorded everyone saying good bye.

SHAUN: (<u>A prayer</u>) Please St. James, guide our wheels and bring us safely to your shrine and to heaven.

SEAMUS: And at 4.10 the train set off. At 6.46 the train arrived at Portsmouth Harbour Station. We cycled one and a half miles to the ferry terminal at about seven o'clock. I'm very excited about having to cycle onto the boat.

(<u>INTERWEAVE SOUND EFFECTS OF SEAGULLS AND SEA WASH</u>)

ACTORS AS MEDIAEVAL FRIENDS OF PILGRIMS:
(<u>Calling</u>) Pray for us at Santiago, May St. James look after you, etc.

SEAMUS: The boat rocked all night, up, down, up, down, and it was awful, but I still liked it.

(<u>SAILING BOAT MAKING GOOD WAY. MEDIAEVAL MUSIC</u>)

ACTOR:
Haul up the bowline, now, veer the sheet!
Cooke make ready our meat,
Our pilgrims have no lust to eat.
Steward a pot of beer!
Anon of the best.

(MIX FROM MEDIAEVAL MUSIC TO
BACKGROUND OF CONTEMPORARY TOURIST
CROWD)

SHAUN:
After docking at St. Malo, we started our
pilgrimage proper from Mont St Michel,
Normandy, where many pilgrims set out in the
Middle Ages.

(ACTUALITY OF GUIDE IN FRENCH)

GUIDE:
Ça commence ici la visite à Mont St. Michel, etc

(FADE AS WE MOVE AWAY)

SEAMUS:
Mont St. Michel was crowded with tourists and
very noisy. We left our bicycles by the
Gendarmerie.

SHAUN:
And walked up the crowded, tripper streets
with our heavy packs to the Abbey.

(LOSE CROWDS. BRING UP A MIXED
COMMUNITY OF MONKS AND NUNS SINGING
PLAIN CHANT IN FRENCH)

SHAUN:
There we were met by Sister Brigitte and
attended vespers. We had a simple Friday
supper and walked round the island with the
tide coming up and we had a good night's
sleep.

(LOSE PLAINCHANT)

Matins at seven o'clock in the small oratory, followed by breakfast and Lauds; and then one of the brothers blessed our undertaking.

BROTHER: Benissez especialment nos deux amis qui maintainent vont partir vers St. Jacques de Compostelle,

(INTRODUCE GENTLE MEDIAEVAL CHIMES)

que l'Apotre et notre coeur les accompagne sur la route et les ramene sains et sauf dans leur foyer, par Jesus Christ, Notre Seigneur, Amen

SHAUN: Amen

SEAMUS: Amen.

This feature was over a year in the making. As you can imagine, cycling up to fifty miles a day with a twelve year old and finding the route and accommodation was a full time activity. We managed to keep diaries however; most of which we recorded on family holiday in France the next summer, just before Seamus' voice broke. A generous and talented colleague, John Theocharis, produced it and provided an objective ear. He was able to tell me where I was self-indulgent and should be cut and where Seamus and I were instructive and entertaining. John Tydeman described the feature as "Pilgrim and Adrian Mole."

9 From Script to Production

Putting Yourself In The Producers' Place

Sometimes the roles of writer and producer may be combined. The playwright, Anthony Minghella co-directed his *Cigarettes and Chocolates* with Radio Drama Producer, Robert Cooper. The result was one of the most moving and magical productions I have ever heard.

I believe, however that this arrangement was an example of the exception that proves the rule. Normally a successful production will be the result of a team effort in which the roles of writer and producer are separate, but complementary.

Just as a good producer should understand the script as thoroughly as possible, so it can help you, the writer to take an imaginative leap and to put yourself in the position of the producer. Identifying the producer's problems, disciplines and aspirations should help you to improve your script, which in the final analysis is the blueprint for the production.

In radio the roles of producer, who has overall control of the programme: management, administration and budgeting, and of the director, who has artistic control, involving such decisions as casting, choice of music and interpretation, are combined.

Finding the Script or Idea

One can do much to ruin a good script, but one cannot, even with magnificent performances, beautiful music, sensitive pacing and creative post-production, make a good play out of an uninspired and derivative script.

Thus the producer's first priority must be to find an outstanding script. Unfortunately a producer's time is finite and he will not be able devote a great deal of attention to every script submitted. In the BBC script Unit in the seventies, six of us considered about 300 unsolicited scripts a week. We had a rule, that all scripts specifically written for radio, that were neither incoherent nor obscene, should receive a short synopsis and

comment.   However to devote time to those that were
comparatively uninspired was to lose spending precious time on
the more promising. We had to make hard decisions. At today's
cost conscious BBC script readers are far more ruthless than we
were.

Independent producers' way of working is not so different
from that of the BBC in-house producers. Attending writers'
seminars, keeping in touch with the writers one knows, teaching
writing courses at universities, coming across talented new writers,
through word of mouth and recommendation and seeing stage
plays, that would adapt well to radio are all ways of finding new
material. One may feel that some plays are not right for radio, but
that the writers show promise and that one should meet them to
discuss further ideas. At the moment I am working on a theatre
production in Vietnam and have come across one or two plays,
that would translate well to British radio.

However I prefer to have ideas and scripts that are thought
of in the first place in terms of radio. My chief hate are rejected
television plays, that a writer thinks 'might' make a radio play.
The two media could not be more different and it can take more
time and creative energy to adapt a television into a radio play,
than to write a new radio play entirely from scratch.

We will examine the tricky problem of how to sell your
script to BBC Broadcast or other outlets in the next chapter.

Script Editing

As producer, having found your proposal or your script, you
should do everything in your power to help the writer to improve
it. However your guiding principle should be to remain true to the
author's intentions. Script Editing then casting, I regard as the two
most vital parts of a producer's job. If you get these right, you can
almost sit back and enjoy the rest of the production.

The trick of a lazy script editor such as myself, who also wants to
be popular and seen as not interfering, is to persuade the writer to
make any changes that are needed. I should never advise a
producer or script editor to re-write somebody else's script; not
even in the unlikely event of a writer begging him to do so.

Timing

Timing the script is important at first draft stage. If it is over long or, more disastrously, under-running for the scheduled slot, then valuable time in the studio and in post-production will be wasted. You will end up with a worse production, than you need have done. It is easy to get the timing wrong. Every writer's dialogue seems, intrinsically, to play at a different pace. How many words there are in a script is irrelevant. The only foolproof way to time a script is to read it aloud with a stopwatch in hand. Allow, generously, for music, sound effects and silences.

Advertising and pronunciation

Two routine matters to consider are those of advertising and pronunciation. The BBC by its charter is not permitted to promote commercial products. Thus strictly speaking product names such as Hoover, Mercedes or Johnny Walker should not be used. If the writer can find an alternative, time may be saved in the studio. The BBC has a pronunciation unit, though I believe in our accountancy mad age, it now charges internally for this service. So again the more the writer can help the producer to research the correct pronunciation of foreign words, place names, technical terms, etc, the more time and money will be saved at production stage.

Strong language

Strong language is a subject discussed *ad nauseam* within the BBC. The point is often made, that in broadcasting a play, you are inviting yourself into the privacy of people's homes and that it is courteous therefore to eschew offensive, ugly or scatological language. On the other hand should one apologise for something that one feels is artistically essential? Also the BBC's policy on this mater are considerably more than even a few years ago

I should add, that in this respect, as in most others, radio works very differently from the visual media. To put it crudely, if you use the word 'fucking' on radio, that, generally speaking, is the activity that you are inviting the listener to visualise. In all other media the language will be counterpointed - or complemented - by what is happening in sight. Thus for good or ill, strong language can be a much more powerful weapon on radio than in other media.

Casting

A writer may start with a particular actor in mind for the leading role. As long as he is prepared to leave the question of casting open as the character and the script develop and as the producer becomes involved, this is not a bad idea. It can sometimes lend an extra dimension and it can serve as shorthand between writer and producer.

Time is always at a premium in the studio. Compared with other media, one has virtually no time for rehearsal; so the actor who is 'right' for the part and who comes to the studio prepared is absolutely vital. If as producer I realise, that an actor has not done sufficient homework, I tend to forget him when it comes to future casting. Fortunately there are too many dedicated and talented actors competing for work, to leave room for those who are careless or lazy.

I admit, that because studio time is at such a premium, I tend to cast 'safely' and to use those actors who I already know well. One's first responsibility is to the listener, then to the writer and only then to the actors.

I find I generally cast well, when I 'listen' to the play at my first reading. It is then that I tend to hear the voices. In fact, it is almost as if someone else does the casting.

I sometimes confuse actors by saying: 'You'd better ask the other Shaun MacLoughlin for a part.' If my first choice of actor is may not be available, then I start to agonise. It is crucial to get the casting right.

Budgeting

Many costs are fixed. There is little room for manoeuvre over the price of the studio, the editing channels, the technicians' hourly rates, copyright payment. The last is by agreement between the broadcasting organisations and the Society of Authors and The Writers' Guild. Thus the variables, upon which pressure is invariably exerted, are the size of the cast and the length of time required for recording and post-production. There is a growing tendency not to use drama studios, which are expensive to rent, especially in London, but to record on location.

The cost of post-production comes down fairly radically, if one invests in the appropriate computer software and learns to operate it oneself. However this can be time consuming, while artistically one may loses the objectivity provided by another pair of ears.

I normally persuade writers to keep the play technically as simple as possible. On the other hand I try to avoid allowing budgetary pressures to inhibit artistic pioneering and an innovative and experimental use of the medium.

At my second reading I work out how to schedule scenes, so that I can record out of order to save on actors' days. It is particularly important, when, for example, I am bringing actors from London to Bristol, to save on hotel and travel expenses. I also work out possible doubling. Opposite is an example of a schedule for *A Midsummer Night's Dream*. I enjoyed the fantasy casting.

This exercise is almost entirely to save on the budget. Patrick Stewart and Bill Wallis will not be required on Friday or Saturday and all the 'mechanicals', except Bottom, will not be required on the Saturday. Supposing Christian Rodska, playing Snout, is offered a day's filming or voice over work on the Thursday, then he can be released. The only time we should have the entire cast together would be for the read-through.

DREAM – Casting Schedule. Read-through Mon 6, Record Tue 7 to Sat 11 Sept 2004

Act/Scene		1.1	1.2	5.1	4.1	4.2	3.1	3.2	2.1	2.2
Length										162
DAY		TUE	TUE	WED	THUR	THUR	FRI	FRI	SAT	SAT
Theseus	Patrick Stewart	TH		TH	TH					
Egeus	Bill Wallis	EG			EG					
Lysander	Robert Glenister	LY		LY	LY			LY		LY
Demetrius	Iain Glen	DE		DE	DE			DE	DE	DE
Philostrate/Snug/Lion	Timothy West		SNU	PH/S		SNU	SNU			
Quince/Prologue	Bob Hoskins		QU	QU		QU	QU			
Bottom/Pyramus	Anthony Hopkins		BT	BT	BT	BT	BT			BT
Flute/Thisbe	Tony Robinson		FL	FL		FL	FL			
Snout/Wall	Christian Rodska		SNO	SNO		SNO	SNO			
Starveling/Moon	Cornelius Garrett		ST	ST		ST	ST		PE	
Hippolyta/Peasebloss	Juliet Stevenson	HP		HP	HP/P	PE	PE			PE
Hermia/Cobweb	Carolyn Backhouse	HR			HR/C	HR/C	CO	HR		HR/C
Helena/Mustardseed	Jenny Funnel	HL			H/M	HL/M	MU	HL	OB	HL/M
Oberon	Alan Rickman			OB	OB	OB		OB	OB	OB
Titania/Moth	Kate Beckinsale			TI	TI	TI/MO	T/M		TI	T/MO
Puck	Jean-Mar Perret			PU	PU	PU	PU	PU	PU	PU

Organising Publicity And Promotion

In the rush and business of production, this is often an important job that gets overlooked. It is a great pity as, if radio drama had enjoyed a higher profile over the past twenty years, it might now have a brighter future.

Within the BBC, part of one's routine as a producer is to compile a Promotion Note, with information about star casting and anything else that is newsworthy.   This goes to the Channel Controller, who decides whether the programme should be given promotion and publicity priority as the lead of the day or of the week.   The best publicity will always emanate from the personal enthusiasm of those actually working on the programme, who will understand its intentions, have first hand knowledge and commitment and may well spot an unusual and attractive publicity angle.

Since I have left the BBC I have found a few phone calls to journalist friends, accompanied with an invitation to sit in on the studio production, has more than paid dividends.   If you are promoting and selling plays on the Internet, the design and 'information architecture' of WEB pages is particularly important.

Incorporating Music

We have covered the use of commercial recordings earlier.   Some composers will write for live musicians.   Others will create electronic music in their own studio. In either case the producer should receive a rough draft of the music before going into the studio, so that he can then gauge, during the recording, how the music will match the performances. Usually the music will be dubbed on afterwards, leaving the producer and editor to fine tune the right levels. Ideally I like to feed the music to the leading actor through headphones so that he can time and adjust his performance to the music, while allowing me to control the relative volume of speech and music in post-production.

Using Sound Effects

The BBC has a vast library of pre-recorded sound effects, while many independent studios are building up similar collections. Students on media courses often go out with DAT recorders and create their own sound effects.   It is important, that whatever facilities one does or does not have, one prepares this as much as possible before recording in the studio.

Some years ago I produced *God's Revolution* by Don Taylor, an original 12 episode Classic Serial about Cromwell and the Levellers. It contained numerous battle scenes, mostly on horse back. We recorded horse-riding effects deep in the countryside, away from traffic. We had to achieve single horses and groups of horses, starting from standing still and then galloping, trotting and walking away on soft and on hard surfaces. We had to record travelling with the horse - or horses. We had to record the horses arriving and stopping, both from the point of view of a rider and from the point of view of the person being approached. It was a long day's work, but a healthy and enjoyable one.

Champagne and its possible after-effects

The other kind of sound effects are live or 'spot effects' that one creates physically in the studio. My favourite sequence is opening a bottle of champagne and pouring it out into a glass and then, perhaps a little later, being sick.

If the budget does not run to several bottles of bubbly (for re-takes), one uses a sawn off bicycle pump with a cork stuffed into it, that one then pumps and pops out. At the same time that one pours water into a glass, close to the mike, one adds Alka Seltzer or Beachams Powder to create the necessary fizz.   To create the effect of being sick, one needs a hot water bottle filled with water, but without the stopper. The actor clasps it to his chest and then leans forward, making a retching noise as he goes, until with perfect timing and appropriate movement the contents slurp onto the floor.

The Planning Meeting

It can be a good idea, particularly on a complex production to have a planning meeting with the technicians to discuss the overall approach and in particular any special sound effects required. One needs to be aware that some technicians, particularly those comparatively new to Radio Drama, may be over literal about sound effects. They may not realise, the actual noise of say a car swerving, will not create the required image in the listener's mind. This needs very careful thought. A technician may say to me, 'But this is a recording of a Rolls Royce,' when all one hears is a gentle hum that could evoke almost anything. Sometimes one needs to explain, that because the play stipulates one is in a busy London street, one does not want to hear a continuous heavy noise of traffic, drowning out all nuances of a conversation. In real life, subjectively, we often block out such noises from our consciousness.

At the planning meeting one can also discuss the overall schedule in the studio and any unusual approaches, one wishes to take. If one intends to record all or any of the play on location, careful and thorough planning is needed to find the right locations, organise transport to and fro, and have fall back, contingency plans in case of violent, i.e. noise-making rain or continuous interruptions by unwanted other noises. Incidentally a pretty and charming actress, to persuade a farm labourer to leave his tractor and go for a pint of cider, can be a real asset.

Preparing The Actors

If there is a particular problem for an actor, such as difficult pronunciations, an unusual accent or an ambiguity in the script, then a letter or phone call may save considerable time in the studio. You may wish to give them some background information that is not contained in the script. With these problems the playwright should be able to help. In any case, it is vital to get the script to the actors as early as you can, so that they have ample preparation time.

Some star actors require a degree of cosseting. They may like a car to collect them and if they are staying in a hotel, make sure they are well looked after and feel loved.

Such care on the part of the producer and production assistant can pay real dividends.   It is vital to create a happy working atmosphere in the studio.

Getting Into The Studio

At last the preparation is over and the most enjoyable part of the production can begin. The studio is divided into the control room, from where the main part of the production team will monitor and record the play; and the studio proper, a series of sound proof acoustic spaces, where the actors and floor manager will operate. There will also be a 'green room' for the actors to relax in between takes.

For many years I was fortunate to work at Christchurch Drama Studio Bristol. This is a magical and inspiring building, that in its time has been a brewery warehouse, a village school and a Church of England hall. The entire building is wired for microphones, talk-back and cue lights. I once, illegally, used the air conditioning unit to record a shoot out in a container ship. It had the right acoustic. There is a fully practical kitchen, which with the window open to the resonant courtyard at the side of the studio. I have used this combination to record scenes in a fishmonger's. The cellars with their connecting stairs and corridors are marvellous for Shakespearean dungeons and Nazi-torture chambers. Best of all is the 'dead room' or anachoic chamber, where outdoor scenes are recorded. (It is called 'dead', because the acoustic is not 'live' or echoey, but absorbent.) There is an 'acoustic trap', a padded bending corridor, leading off the dead room, in which one can create war cries and cavalry charges approaching from half a mile away. This studio is an inspiration to all, who work there and greatly loved throughout the profession. It now belongs to the Bristol Old Vic Theatre School who are happy to rent it out.

The Production Team

The production team consists of the Producer; the Production Assistant who keeps a record of the timing of each scene, of how many 'takes' there may be and of any 'fluffs' and 'go-backs' (to cover an edit) by the actors; the Senior Studio Manager who operates the mixing desk and is responsible to the producer for all technical matters; and the Grams Op., who is responsible for playing in music and recorded sound effects and for monitoring, that the play is recorded. If time permits, the Grams Op. may also assemble the chosen takes and begins on the post production; as the producer is rehearsing the next scene. The final member of the production team is the Floor Manager, who works with the actors in the studio. She is responsible for calling the actors from the green room and for creating, or for delegating the actors to create, the practical, 'spot' effects.

Recently the BBC has tended to economise on production personnel and there is a growing tendency to double up on some of the above functions.

The writer's role

The writer is usually invited to be present in the control room. It is the mark of a good producer to use the writer as constructively as possible; in fact as part of the production team. After all it is the writer who has first 'heard' the play and who should have a great deal of value to contribute. However it is to the play's and therefore the writer's advantage to remember that the play cannot be produced by committee. Time is in short supply in the studio and one person can direct the actors and technicians without creating confusion.

Rehearsing and Recording

There are two basic ways to rehearse and record a radio play. The more common is called 'Rehearse / Record'. This means breaking the play down into convenient, recordable sequences, preferably, but not necessarily, in the order of the play and then rehearsing and recording each sequence in turn.

The other way is to rehearse the entire play first and then to record it in one go; or at least in as long sequences as are technically feasible to accomplish. Different producers and actors prefer different methods. I tend to use the first method, because I work mostly in Bristol and, in say a three day production, my budget may only stretch to some London based actors for one or two days. I may therefore have to record the scenes affecting those actors out of sequence. Many actors prefer this method as it means total concentration for shorter, intenser periods. They can relax between takes. Others however favour recording the play in a single go. They feel that by taking a sweep at it, it can sometimes take off in a way that achieves unexpected depths and greater emotional intensity.

The Read-Through

In either case I am a passionate believer in the importance of the read-through. This is when the actors with the producer, the writer and the production assistant sit down and read the play together for the first time. The technicians may be present, though they may need to set up the studio and 'build the sets' during this period.

The Read-Through may be the only opportunity before the final edit to hear the play in its entirety. It is a crucial occasion for the actors to 'offer' their interpretation; for the production assistant to time the play; and for the writer and the producer to respond.

Over the years as a producer, I have tended to say less and less before the Read-Through. Some of my colleagues give the most brilliant, erudite and fascinating exposés of the script. However I feel that, if I say too much, I may inhibit an actor from offering an interesting and valuable interpretation, that neither the writer nor I have foreseen.

After the Read-Through, with reference to the writer, I hope to give the most crucial notes. It may often be a case of two leading actors offering a very different interpretation, so that they hardly appear to be in the same play. A compromise has to be sought. There may be some background information, an anecdote about a person or place or the writer's motive for writing the play, that the actors will find enlightening. The appropriateness of accents, particularly where an actor has to double or treble parts, may need to be examined. The few minutes after the read-through can be a very fertile period.

A paradoxical problem occurs, when an actor gives, what one considers, a perfect reading. Actors like something to chew upon. They like to feel they are progressing, that they have somewhere to go; so it is not actually very helpful to tell them, that what they have done is perfect and to ask them simply to repeat themselves. I therefore always try to say something to them, even if it is upon a minor point of information or a quibble about the pronunciation of a single word.

Generally criticism must be constructive. There simply is not time in the studio to break an actor's confidence and then to build it up again. I remember the story of a dear colleague, who miscast a part disastrously. During a rehearsal when he was producing from the control room, he put his head in hands in despair, murmured, 'Oh my God!' took a deep breath, went out into the studio and lied enthusiastically: 'That was absolutely wonderful, darling! Now let's build on it: point 1..... point 2..... point 3..... point 4....'

I like, if possible, to have the first lunch break after the Read-Through to give the actors - and myself and the writer - time to mull over what has passed and what we want to achieve. Ideally I like to have the read-through the day before recording. That is not always possible, simply for budgetary reasons; but artistically to allow a night to sleep on the Read-Through can be invaluable.

Once the Rehearse/Record proper begins, some producers will tend to rehearse in the studio, where they can relate more directly to the actors. Others will stay in the control room, where they can relate more directly to the listener - and to the writer and the technicians. I tend to play it by ear and vary my approach, but I think that as producer my primary function is to identify with the listener. (I often keep my eyes closed). In fact I have to attempt to be a sort of 'archetypal' listener. I may even invite a sympathetic visitor to the studio to share this function.

Reacting to the Rehearsal

If I listen from the control room, at the end of a scene's rehearsal, I press the talk back button, thank the actors and tell them I shall shortly be with them.

I then digest as quickly as possible the writer's and the senior studio manager's reactions. Generally I do not invite the writer to speak directly to the actors as this can consume too much precious time. Also the writer may not be practised in how to get the best out of the actors. Armed with my own thoughts and those of my colleagues, I then, hastily, think how to translate these into constructive notes and so I enter the studio.

Knowing what not to say is as important as knowing what to say. I try to keep my notes to a minimum. I like to leave 'space' for the actors to be creative. Also time is at a premium in the studio. One is always working against the clock to get the best results.

After I have given the actors their notes, I generally go for the first take. Although this may be a little early, it will tend to concentrate minds and energies. I often find at this stage, that in their performance, I can hear the actors thinking about the notes, I have given them. They may be on the right lines, but sound a little stilted. I therefore thank them very nicely and ask them to have another go, making the notes their own. At this second take I usually find one elicits the best performance, that one is liable to get within the limited time at one's disposal. Often at this point the actors discover a spontaneity and energy; they catch the character, as it were, upon the wing. If one had days to rehearse as in most other media, one might come back to and surpass this point. However I usually find that, if one flogs a scene too much, staleness sets in.

If I have time, I go back towards the end of, the recording period, to the opening of the play and re-record it. By then the actors should be more deeply into their characters and be able to offer something more compelling.

Different producers will have very different approaches and the more producers that you as a writer can work with the better. You may grow to totally disagree with what I have just said and, if you do, I am sure it will be very healthy.

Location Drama

Particularly in London with the rising cost of studios, there is a growing tendency to record on location. A 'dry' studio, that is one without technicians, can cost at least a £1,000 a day; whereas on location one has only the cost of a portable recorder - and possibly added transport and catering costs.

This is generally only appropriate in contemporary plays, because there are few locations completely free of the sound of distant traffic, farm machinery or the flight path of aeroplanes. Even with a play in a modern setting one may be subject to time consuming interruptions adding to the pressure and budget. (I do know of one or two deep valleys, near Bristol, that are almost always quiet.)

When things are working well as they did for me when I recorded *Whee' Oss* by R.E.T. Lamb, a play set in Padstow in Cornwall on Mayday, the result can be magical. The actors found themselves inspired by the setting and one was able to achieve a sense of space, which in the studio, even with Christchurch Studio's acoustic trap, would have been impossible. We recorded one scene at night in a garden about half a mile from the distant celebrations in the fishing town. There was a sense of holiness in the air and the actors instinctively lowered their voices. I don't think I would have thought to have given them that direction in the studio.

The first play that I recorded entirely on location was by the poet and travel writer, Paul Hyland. It was called *Dancing Ledge*, named after an artificial cave quarried out of the rock on the Purbeck peninsular in Dorset. We had actors running in and out of the echoey cave, calling to each other on a ledge just above the sea. This was something else that could not have been achieved in the studio.

My favourite location moment was in Australia. I recorded in the national park, south of Sydney, a scene about 19th Century White Australian gold diggers beating up Chinese coolies. It was an improvised scene and one inspired Australian actor went tearing off into the bush, pursuing an imaginary coolie and yelling, in a very politically incorrect manner, 'Ching-Chong-Chinaman.'

At this precise moment a kookaburra chose to let off its mocking, unearthly laugh. It was the end of the scene and I was worried that my friend Andrew, the BBC technician, had faded out too early, but he gave me the thumbs up.

Peter Terson wrote a series of what he called 'landscape plays', in which we developed a technique of mixing studio and location. For example scenes in the chief character's memory or in his fantasy might take place in the abstract, controlled setting of the studio with only remembered or imagined sound effects, while scenes in the present storyline might take place on location with the more intrusive and accidental sounds of the everyday world. This technique gave a nice variety and contrast to the texture of the play.

Post-Production

I generally find that recording is a euphoric time and post-production or editing is a deeply depressing experience. It is then, as producer, that one hears all the mistakes one has made; all the notes one has *not* given to the actors and technicians.

However I have to come to realise, that this also is the time to use one's depression professionally, to rectify one's mistakes as much as possible. It is remarkable what one can achieve with state of the art, digital, editing software and the speed with which one can do it. One can change the actors' timing and their level or 'presence'. One can dub on music and sound effects. One can even, up to a point, play with the pitch, 'the top' or 'bottom' or modify the stereo 'picture' to lessen the effects of over obtrusive or unwanted sound effects. However this all takes valuable and expensive time and it is, of course, better not to have made such mistakes in the first place.

10 Marketing Your Script

Writing For The BBC

The BBC remains the guardian of the great British tradition of Radio Drama. This alone is a strong argument for the retention of the BBC's independence and of the license fee. A free nation speaks to itself through the original voices of its story tellers. I may hold an eccentric view on this subject, but I truly believe that the loss of the regular single original play on TV was a tragedy and that the survival of the original play on BBC Radio is important to our democracy.

Certain writer unfriendly measures were introduced during the director generalship of John Birt. However Greg Dyke did wonders to restore staff morale and it is to be hoped that, in spite of his departure, this will lead to a more positive and regular response to writers' proposals. Let us hope that sooner rather than later a weekly response to writers' submissions will be reinstated, that this particular wheel be reinvented. This could only improve the standard of radio drama.

The Controller's View

However I am pleased to report that the quality and quantity of BBC radio drama and staff morale are showing signs of recovery. When I made enquiries for this edition my ex-colleagues were positive and helpful. Helen Boaden, Controller Radio 4 wrote:

> "We do a huge amount of Drama and inevitably, some of it falls short of what we had hoped for…I want Radio Drama to continue to flourish…One of our great challenges is to woo new listeners - many of whom have not grown up with speech radio as their first medium - into the pleasures of Radio Drama. Our Drama output has to chime with the intelligence and curiosity of our listeners and should offer a diversity of style, format and content which I know our audience expects. It is incredibly important that writers for Radio 4 listen across the Network and understand the very broad range of interests and tastes that we serve…. It is

important that we maintain a balance between new writing and established writers who have an instinctive feel for Radio 4."

Kate Rowland, Head of the New Writing Initiative adds:

"Radio Drama has a real commitment to new writers. The Wire on R3 represents the best of new contemporary writing - the network is constantly looking to reflect drama as it happens - writers at the forefront - bold, popular storytellers. We are committed to represent a diversity of voices."

Choosing your programme slot

The following are subject to change, but provide an idea of what the BBC is looking for. Radio 4's Commissioning Editor's comments are as follows:

"Woman's Hour Drama 15' daily serial: Dramatisations and new work, not a slot for beginners. Afternoon Play. 45'. single plays with occasional series: new work, dramatisations, drama documentaries, mysteries, thrillers, crime and biographical pieces. Friday Play. 60' single works that test the medium. Unlikely to be place for beginners unless they have track record in either theatre or film or television. Saturday Play 60' single plays with strong narrative. Crime, romance, mysteries and thrillers encouraged. Classic Serial. 60' serialisations of extant works of fiction. Not a slot for beginners. Writers interested in this area should check with Commissioning Editor's office at Radio 4 whether the title is already under commission or has been recently broadcast."

There is also comedy on Radio 4: *Monday-Friday 11.30- 12.00.* Narrative. Reviving, energising and cheery. *Monday-Thursday 18.30-19.00.* Sitcom, broken comedy or sketch shows. Family entertainment. *Friday 18.30.* Satire. *Tuesday, Wednesday and*

Thursday 23.00-23.30. Top comedy performers and writers. New comic ideas and forms. Sharp wit and intelligence rather than surreal. *Children's Drama.* It is rumoured (*Whitaker's Almanac 2001*) that Radio 4 will be reviving some.

On Radio 3 the *Sunday Play* consists of major classics, "radical plays" and new theatre plays. This is the only regular slot for full length plays on radio. There is a new experimental writing slot called *The Wire* on the first Thursday of the month, for which Kate Rowland is responsible as she is for the *Friday Play* on Radio 4.

Submitting your scripts

Since the last edition of this book the BBC has created a very helpful online resource for writing for television, radio and film See: http://www.bbc.co.uk/writersroom. One of the values of this website is that information is continuously updated. It "brings you information about writing opportunities and events, along with useful tips and advice from, and interviews with professional writers and other industry experts." There you will also out how to lay out your script, what information is required with it and who to submit it to. Equally I recommend the guidelines on Radio Entertainment. I paraphrase its valuable advice:

Before you even set a finger to keyboard, there are a few golden rules that will prevent you from wasting your time, and ours:

Know your market. Listen and find out what you like and don't like. The frequencies and schedules are available in the national press or the Radio Times. Remember, everything you hear has been chosen by the controller of that network, who also must ultimately buy your idea; remember also that the core audience of Radio 2 and radio 4 are in their 50s.

If you want to write a sitcom, find a situation that hasn't been covered recently. However, there's no point in simply trying to 'find a gap in the market'. You have to feel some genuine passion.

Try and find your own voice. Just as many new bands sound exactly like their heroes, we get lots of work from new writers that reads exactly like Chris Morris or *Monty Python* or *The Goon Show*. Ask yourself: 'Am I the only person in the world who could have written like this?'

How writers respond to criticism is a key aspect of their development, and is always taken into account by producers. Writing the same kind of thing in the same kind of way, hoping that one day you'll get lucky, doesn't work.

Another way to submit your script is to find a sympathetic producer. To do this listen to as many productions as possible and decide, which producers' taste and style seem appropriate to your work. If they like it, they in turn will have to submit your script to a commissioning editor, but at least you will have a friend and an advocate at court. The added advantage of doing this is that you gain considerable insight in to what the BBC are producing and you may spot some gaps in the output that you might help to plug.

You will see from the BBC's guidelines that if you live in one of the BBC regions, such as the Midlands (Birmingham), the North (Manchester), Northern Ireland, Scotland or Wales you are encouraged to submit your script to a producer in your area.

Bristol's documentary feature making department is interested in drama with a documentary side to it that uses poetry or has a literary aspect. Unless you are offering ideas, which fall into these areas this is not an ideal place to submit your work. Producers are Jeremy Howe, Tim Dee, Viv Beeby, Sara Davies, Paul Dodgson, Mary Ward Lowery and Kate McAll. However check first that you can find their names in the Radio-Times, as producers do tend to move around

Finally 10% of the Radio Drama is by independent producers. For a full list of those companies who are registered to supply radio drama to Radio 4 go to www.bbc.co.uk/commissioning/structure and click on radio4. A search there should take you to PDF page, which gives companies, contacts and the slots they supply.

Oneword And IRDP

Oneword the national commercial digital radio speech channel was launched in 2001. You can listen online at www. online.co.uk. In January 2004 it had 61,000 listeners, having lost some to BBC7. Most of its output consists in the broadcast of audio publishers' readings. However unlike the BBC it is to be commended on having at least 23 hours of children's broadcasting a week. As we go to press there are plans afoot to change the station's format in an attempt to drive up audience levels. When the station started three years ago there were great plans to introduce radio drama. Let us hope that these will feature in Oneword's new plans.

Independent Radio Drama Production (IRDP) is no longer streaming or producing drama; but it maintains an informative website at www.irdp.co.uk, which contains some perceptive and witty comments from Tim Crook on the do's and don'ts of radio writing.

11 Other forms of Audio Drama and its Future

At present the BBC provides the only viable market for your radio script. However should you wish to explore other ways of writing and producing radio drama or features here are some suggestions. Just as I have chosen examples of writing that I have produced, so here I have also drawn from my own experience. Hopefully you will be able to emulate and surpass what colleagues and I have achieved. In each case friends and colleagues and I had to find funding or a commission and for some of these projects we have had to invest in basic equipment and audio editing software.

Radio Drama For Children

Radio 5 started with a brave experiment to concentrate on children's broadcasting. However this commitment to forming the listening habits of the next generation was shelved in favour of attracting a larger adult audience for 24 four hour news and sport. Now the only regular BBC slot for children on Radio 4 is on Sundays at 7.15 p.m. This consists of a magazine programme containing a drama serial. BBC7 has readings for children

However others are making efforts to fill the gap and not only in the UK. Tony Palermo who writes and directs radio plays for <u>The Museum of Television and Radio</u> in Los Angeles and New York is dedicated to radio drama for children. He writes:

> "There are two different animals: radio drama to be listened to by children and drama performed by children. I work with both and actually specialize in 'frankensteining' them together. Over the last 5 years I've had 20 of my radio workshop plays performed by thousands of kids, aged 9-14. I've even written radio plays to be performed by 5-6 year olds--and they can't read scripts! I'm also the father of an 8 year old and two 5 year olds. Writing for children is a different genre than writing for adults, but not a lesser one. See Mark Twain's Huckleberry Finn if you doubt me."

Radio Drama as Education and Fun

Thanks to a cultural diversity grant from the Arts Council Wales, Tom Bennett and I have recently been doing some of Tony Palermo's 'frankensteining'. We have conducted workshops, in which Cardiff primary school children write and act in their own radio plays – and even create many of the sound effects

We managed with essential input from the class teachers to achieve each of these plays in two half days sessions plus editing and playbacks. We found that mornings were better for the sessions, as the children were more alert. We arrived at the schools by 8 a.m. to set up microphones in one class room and recording equipment in another; thus creating the separation between studio and control room that we would have in a professional recording studio. We built a tent of blankets and duvets, a 'dead' acoustic, around the microphone, ready to work with the children from just after 9 a.m.

During the course of the first morning sessions we had warm up exercises by the third – female – member of our group, an encouraging drama teacher or student. We then played three short excerpts from children's radio plays: *Alice Through the Looking Glass, The Just So Stories* and E. Nesbitt's *The Magic Circle.* We then provided the children with scripts and got them to perform in front of the microphone. Tom recorded and monitored the recordings, our drama teacher shepherded the children and helped them make sound effects and I directed their acting. Finally we played back what they had done.

Throughout this process we asked them for ideas and incidents for radio plays. These we wrote up on the classroom whiteboard and started to storyboard the children's inspirations. We then left the class teacher and the children to complete the scripts over the period of the next ten days or so.

At the second session we returned to record the plays. Since we could not cast every child in classes of up to twenty five, we got many of them to draw pictures and to write short descriptions to accompany the recordings of the plays on our website. This way everybody could feel involved.

Tom then edited the plays and the most rewarding part of the exercise was to return to the schools for a playback, and to present the children with CD's of their achievements.

To date we have recorded three plays of about 15 minutes each: *A Mischievous Fairy* at St Mary's Primary School, Bute Town *The Dreams of Martin Luther King* at Mount Stuart Primary School and *Tornado to Oakenworld* at St. Cuthbert's Catholic Primary School.

You should be able to listen to these online by going to www.soundplay.co.uk/projects and clicking on Cultural Diversity. To give you an idea of what to expect, here is an excerpt from *A Mischievous Fairy.*

ANNOUNCER: We present the "A Mischievous Fairy" a play by Class 5, St Mary's, Bute Town.

NARRATOR: I would like to tell you a story about my mischievous granddaughter called Zelda. This is a story that is told to young fairies like yourselves all over the fairy kingdom by their parents as a warning; a warning that to meddle in other people's business only leads to trouble and strife. Now sit back all of you, make yourselves comfortable and listen carefully. Are you ready?

CHILDREN: Yes we are.

WIND AND WIND CHIMES

NARRATOR: It was not so long ago when Zelda was sitting on her cloud minding her own business. She had been there for nearly two hundred years and was now almost a grown up. One morning Zelda woke up and everything was different. She felt zingy, she felt springy, in fact she felt positively tingly. The reason for this sudden change? Well the delivery of her magic powers, of course

ZELDA: I'm sick of sitting on this cloud. I wish something exciting would happen. It's so boring. I need to have some fun. I've got an idea. I think I'll put my magical powers to some use. I'm sure I'll think of something. I'm out of here

NARRATOR: And with that Zelda had the most mischievous idea ever.

ZELDA: I think I'll play those silly humans on earth a visit. I could have lots of funning playing magical tricks on them.

MAGIC NOISE

NARRATOR: So off Zelda flew, down through the sky towards the earth
ZELDA'S NAUGHTY LAUGHTER

NARRATOR: Laughing like she's never laughed before

ZELDA: Huh, this'll be real fun. Hah, I can see Bob the butcher. He's always nasty and mean to his customers, I think I'll teach him a little lesson.

CHILDREN: What happened next? Quickly, tell us!

The play continues with all the naughty tricks that the children of St. Mary's could dream up. Zelda clicks her magic fingers and a pack of dogs gobble up Bob's sausages. She drops squidgy pies on the baker's face and eggs on to the mayor's head and turns tea into jelly. She glues a courting couple's lips together. At the dentist's she has all Mrs Morgan's teeth drop out. The sound effects of teeth falling into a basin were graphic and the girl playing Mrs Morgan gave an excellent imitation of being toothless. Zelda turns greedy children into squeaking, grunting pigs. At the hairdressers Zelda transforms customers' hair into spaghetti. Eventually, tired after so much fun, she goes to sleep on a lily pad, where she is caught by some naughty children and put in a jam jar – a good acoustic. When she wakes up her magic has run out. She has to stay there for two hundred years thinking up more tricks for the next time she will get her magic power again.

Christian Roberts the class teacher at Mount Stuart described the writing of *The Dreams of Martin Luther King* from his and the children's perspective:

> "The children were curiously excited as they entered the class. Lots of radio equipment had taken the place of the plastic books/pens/ruler boxes and this increased the excited chatter. Steph, the student teacher, and I calmed the kids and introduced them to Shaun, Tom and Jesse. Initially they were slow to join in, but as Shaun described that they could create pretty much anything, their ideas began to flow. Tom showed them how to create the sound of wind and they began to fire questions and suggestions as to how they also could create many different sounds.
>
> The kids then listened to excerpts of radio plays, and began to suggest ideas of an almost stream of conscious supply. Their ideas were excellent and the best were incorporated into the play.
>
> The children benefited from this project, by learning that through imagination, language and sound effects they can translate their dreams and ideas into a finished production, which they can keep as a record of their achievement."

Damien Murphy the class teacher at St. Cuthbert's also summed up the value of the exercise:

> "Involving the children in radio drama has been an absolute dream. Not only was I able to combine the National Curriculum literacy demands of speaking and listening, writing and reading, it has also given the children a first hand insight into the world of entertainment and media. It has given them self worth and self esteem.
>
> The advantages of radio over television in developing imagination cannot be overstated. Too many children today

are forced to be the passive receivers of others' images. Creating a radio play on CD and on the Internet, professionally arranged and recorded, has enabled the children to celebrate their success.

Their families, friends and the wider community have marvelled at what the children have achieved in working with others. This fosters not only confidence, but positive social reinforcement, which is so needed in some of our societies today."

Radio Drama And Features In Prison

One of the advantages of radio as opposed to film is that it can be a cost effective way for a community to participate in the creative process of educating, informing and entertaining; and to produce a finished result in a short time. Producing plays and features with prisoners, their families and friends and staff has proved to be another socially beneficial use of radio.

I have been fortunate in working with Mary Stephenson, who was Writer in Residence at Her Majesty's Prison, Channings Wood, Newton Abbott. She wrote a play from life about a bare-knuckle boxer, who had been sentenced for murder and whose girl friend had given birth just after his imprisonment. His girlfriend then married another man, but the growing relationship of the prisoner with his son was very moving. The prisoner played himself and Nicole Tongue, a student actress, cleared along with myself to enter the prison, played his son. Staff and other inmates were effective in playing themselves. The result was broadcast on the prison radio.

We also worked with the prison's Drugs Therapeutic Community to put together three twenty minutes radio features with the overall title of *A Journey through Drugs*. These were compiled from interviews with the prisoners and their families, friends and staff, also with their poems, music and songs composed and performed and improvised dramas. Part one was *The First Fix*, part two *The Depths* and part three *Rehabilitation*.

This won the radio category of the Arthur Koestler award for creative work in prisons. One of the judges wrote:

"This was outstanding in every way. I was moved, appalled and saddened by the tragedies I heard. You educated and informed me and I can only say I feel encouraged that you are working together to start new lives. My admiration is boundless and I cannot congratulate you enough."

After the opening credits *The First Fix* started:

(ELECTRONIC MUSIC SWELL AND TAKE UNDER)

YOUNG DRUG USER:

I take drugs for fun. I don't take drugs to become completely and utterly disassociated from reality. Do you know hat I mean? I'm in control of it – definitely.

INMATE 1: At times I knew I had a problem, but because it wasn't affecting me really, I didn't realise I was a Junkie, like people see a junkie with needles hanging out of their arms and whatever. It was summat I thought I could handle, but I realised it was stopping me progress in life basically.

SWELL DREAMY, EXOTIC ELECTRONIC MUSIC AND TAKE UNDER:

STUDENT ACTRESS: (reading from Thomas De Quincey's *Confessions of an English Opium-eater*)

Oh just, subtle and all conquering opium that to the hearts of rich and poor alike bringest an assuaging balm. Eloquent opium!
Thou buildest upon the bosom of darkness, out of the fantastic imageries of the brain, cities and temples beyond the splendours of Babylon and from the anarchy of dreaming sleep call'st into sunny light the faces of long buried beauties. Thou hast the keys of paradise.

(SWELL MUSIC AND LOSE)

INMATE 2:   Next time I took, it in was in Bombay, in India. I met this French prostitute and her fellow who was selling heroin at two pound a gram. I thought give us a go of that like.

Two students from Dartington Hall then explained how they draw on the life experiences of prisoners to help them create improvised dramas, which I then directed for radio. Thus we introduced a 90 second playlet about becoming a drug addict. Then we interwove further interviews (in which the interviewer was always edited out), poems, songs and more drama to tell the story of how many drug addicts become hooked.

With both programmes recorded at Channings Wood we had to undergo stringent security procedures and work within strictly circumscribed hours. Also as we were working 'on location' we had to be very patient in working round interruptions. We usually used the prison chapel for recording as it was carpeted and less echoey than most of the assembly rooms, corridors or cells. Occasionally we recorded outside in the prison precincts. After recording we edited in the prison studio with prisoners, who were learning to use the prison radio's audio editing software. Other prisons are now interested in doing similar work. You can listen to the result by going to: www.soundplay.co.uk/programmes; click on features.

Paradoxically I discovered that making radio programmes in prison imbued me with a wonderful sense of freedom. I think it was because the exercise released the prisoners' imaginations. It could take the prisoners anywhere and I shared their journey with them.

As we go to press we have applied for a grant to produce the first prison soap opera. Who knows where that might take us?

Audio Guides

Another growing area is the compilation of CDs, audio cassettes and other delivery systems that visitors can listen to while walking round towns, museums, zoos or wherever. These take meticulous preparation; for as well as being informative and entertaining, the instructions of how to play, pause, wind back, etc have to be crystal clear and accurately timed. However they can be great fun to write and to produce, as I discovered when commissioned to make one for the Market Town Initiative at Beccles in Suffolk

We employed two experienced radio actors and obtained quotes from local characters. Here is an excerpt:

ACTRESS: Now enter the tower and mount the narrow spiral staircase to the ringing chamber. Beccles is renowned throughout Suffolk for its peal of ten bells. Note the inscription on the jug:

DAVID WOODWARD:

When I am filled with liquor strong
Each man drink once, and then ding dong
Drink not too much to cloud your knobs
Lest you forget to make the bobs

ACTOR: That was the voice of David Woodward a lover of Beccles and author of *Larn yarself silly Suffolk*. Actually the Suffolk word silly comes from the German "selig" and means blessed or innocent. We shall hear from David again.

SHE: Mounting to the top of the building, being careful not to stumble, you can enjoy a magnificent view in every direction. According to the Beccles registry of 1794 this is the finest view in Europe. When you have taken your fill descend into the Churchyard and cross to the balustrade above the river. Remember you need to start with the yellow button and find track 2 when you get to the balustrade. Now press the red stop button.

(TRACK 2 THE CHURCHYARD, THE VIEW AND THE CHURCH PORCH)

SHE: You should now be standing by the balustrade overlooking the River Waveney.

HE: The Waveney used to be a sea estuary and Beccles was a Saxon seaport. The Doomsday Book tells us Beccles had to supply Bury St. Edmunds Abbey with 10,000 herring a year.

When compiling the guide we had to time our walk very precisely and work out, where we should invite the tourists to pause and identify signs and landmarks. We would advise them which side of a street to cross to for the best views and occasionally we added the sound effect of a car horn to warn them to watch out for traffic. All this took much preparation, but as a result we grew to really know and love the little market town of Beccles

The Future

Broadcasting, with its set hours of listening, may, in the next generation, give way to the freedom of choosing what you want to hear, when you want to hear it. The BBC has taken a large step in this direction with much drama online. I recently talked to a millionaire, who said he believed in vision rather than in audience research. He said, 'Do not talk of Radio Drama, let's call it Sound or Audio Drama. That is the future.'

In his book *Visions, How Science Will Revolutionise the 21st Century and Beyond*, Michio Kaku outlines an imaginary day in 2020 AD. At breakfast your personal computer will have printed out a personalised edition of the newspaper by scanning the Internet for whatever items are most likely to interest you. In the near future, the cost of computers will plummet and their effectiveness in accessing information and entertainment will multiply.

Thus if we have an interest in audio drama, we may be able to find it, when we want it out there in the ether - perhaps for a small charge.

In his book *Radio Drama* Tim Crook describes a survey of fifty young writers, who were asked about the advantages of radio drama on the Internet. They enthused about the opportunity to workshop their material and the freedom to listen at any time of the day. Tim Crook explores the educational value of radio dramaturgy in schools, colleges and universities and suggests that educational funding might provide a way forward.

Yuri Rasovsky has been directing radio drama for over thirty years and has recently been described as 'the most honoured Audio Dramatist working in the United States'. He too detects an encouraging sign for audio drama on the Internet. He says that the first step in building an audience is to put out product even though no one is listening to it. He says that these first guys whether they're good or not are going to put out enough activity to attract some attention and they're going to build audiences for the people who are going to be good. Let's hope he is right for listeners, actors, directors and technicians around the world.

Signing Off

Writing this book has been a joy. It has been a celebration of an immensely fulfilling vocation. It has also concentrated my mind on the way forward. With Tom Bennett and other friends I have founded www.soundplay.co.uk. We plan to pioneer Audio-led Internet Drama with creative and interactive visuals that can complement and counterpoint the plays, documentaries, readings and poetry that you are listening to. Occasionally we shall invite you to close your eyes to see whether the pictures are better. If you would like to know more please contact me: shaun@soundplay.co.uk

As I began this book with A.M.D.G., I should like to conclude with the postscript that completed my homework at Jesuit school: L.D.S (Laus Deum Semper) Praise always to God.

Further Reading

The Art of Radio, Donald McWhinnie (Faber and Faber, 1959).
Best Radio Plays of 1978 (Methuen/BBC):
      Richard Harris: *Is it Something I Said?*
      Don Haworth: *Episode on a Thursday Evening,*
      Jill Hyem: *Remember Me,*
      Tom Mallin: *Halt! Who Goes There?*
      Jennifer Phillips: *Daughters of Men,*
      Fay Weldon: *Polaris;*
Best Radio Plays of 1979 (Methuen/BBC):
      Shirley Gee: *Typhoid Mary,*
      Carey Harrison: *I Never Killed my German,*
      Barrie Keeffe: *Heaven Scent,*
      John Kirkmorris: *Coxcomb,*
      John Peacock: *Attard in Retirement,*
      Olwen Wymark: *The Child;*
Best Radio Plays of 1980 (Methuen/BBC):
      Steward Parker: *The Kamikaze Groundstaff Reunion Dinner,*
      Martyn Read: *Waving to a Train,*
      Peter Redgrove: *Martyr of the Hives,*
      William Trevor: *Beyond the Pale;*
Best Radio Plays of 1981 (Methuen/BBC):
      Peter Barnes: *The Jumping Mimuses of Byzantium,*
      Don Haworth: *Talk of Love and War,*
      Harold Pinter: *Family Voices,*
      David Pownall: *Beef,*
      J. P. Rooney: *The Dead Image,*
      Paul Thain: *The Biggest Sandcastle in the World;*
Best Radio Plays of 1982 (Methuen/BBC):
      Rhys Adrian: *Watching the Plays Together,*
      John Arden: *The Old Man Sleeps Alone,*
      Harry Barton: *Hoopoe Day,*
      Donald Chapman: *Invisible Writing,*
      Tom Stoppard: *The Dog it was that Died,*
      William Trevor: *Autumn Sunshine;*
Best Radio Plays of 1983 (Methuen/BBC):
      Wally K. Daly: *Time Slip,*
      Shirley Gee: *Never in my Lifetime,*

Gerry Jones: *The Angels They Grow Lonely,*
Steve May: *No Exceptions,*
Martyn Read: *Scouting for Boys;*
Best Radio Plays of 1984 (Methuen/BBC)
Stephen Dunstone: *Who is Sylvia?*
Robert Ferguson: *Transfigured Night,*
Don Haworth: *Daybreak,*
Caryl Phillips: *The Wasted Years,*
Christopher Russell: *Swimmer,*
Rose Tremain: *Temporary Shelter;* 1
Best Radio Plays of 1985 (Methuen/BBC):
Rhys Adrian: *Outpatient,*
Barry Collins: *King Canute,*
Martin Crimp: *Three Attempted Acts,*
David Pownall: *Ploughboy Monday,*
James Saunders: *Menocchio,*
Michael Wall: *Hiroshima: The Movie;*
Best Radio Plays of 1986 (Methuen/BBC):
Robert Ferguson: *Dreams, Secrets, Beautiful Lies,*
Christina Reid: *The Last of a Dyin' Race,*
Andrew Rissik: *A Man Alone: Anthony,*
Ken Whitmore: *The Gingerbread House,*
Valerie Windsor: *Myths and Legacies;*
Best Radio Plays of 1987 (Methuen/BBC):
Wally K. Daly: *Mary's,*
Frank Dunne: *Dreams of Dublin Bay,*
Anna Fox: *Nobby's Day,*
Nigel D. Moffat: *Lifetime,*
Richard Nelson: *Languages Spoken Here,*
Peter Tinniswood: *The Village Fete;*
Best Radio Plays of 1988 (Methuen/BBC):
Ken Blakeson: *Excess Baggage,*
Terence Frisby: *Just Remember Two Things: It's Not Fair and Don't Be Late,*
Anthony Minghella: *Cigarettes and Chocolate,*
Rona Munro: *The Dirt under the Carpet,*
Dave Sheasby: *Apple Blossom Afternoons;*

Best Radio Plays of 1989 (Methuen/BBC):
  Elizabeth Baines: *The Baby Buggy,*
  Jennifer Johnston: *0 Ananias, Azarias and Misael,*
  David Zane Mairowitz: *The Stalin Sonata,*
  Richard Nelson: *Eating Words,*
  Craig Warner: *By Where the Old Shed Used to Be;*
Best Radio Plays of 1990 (Methuen/BBC):
  Tony Bagley: *The Machine,*
  David Cregan: *A Butler Did It,*
  John Fletcher: *Death and the Tango,*
  Tina Pepler: *Song of the Forest,*
  Steve Walker: *The Pope's Brother;*
Best Radio Plays of 1991 (Methuen/BBC):
  Robin Glendinning: *The Words are Strange,*
  John Purser: *Carver,*
  Tom Stoppard: *In the Native State,*
  Steve Walker: *Mickey Mookey,*
  Craig Warner: *Figure with Meat*
British Radio Drama ed. John Drakakis (Cambridge University Press, 1981) contains chapters on radio plays of Samuel Beckett, Giles Cooper, Susan Hill, Louis MacNeice, Henry Reed, Dorothy Sayers and Dylan Thomas
Collected Shorter Plays of Samuel Beckett includes radio plays: *All That Fall, Embers, Rough for Radio I, Rough for Radio II, Words and Music, Cascando* (Faber, 1989)
Contacts (The Spotlight, London). A useful guide to professional organisations.
Lake Woebegone Days Garrison Keillor (Faber, 1985)
The Man Born to be King Dorothy Sayers (Ignatius Press, San Francisco, 1943)
Prospero and Ariel, D.G. Bridson (Victor Gollancz 1971)
Radio Acting, Alan Beck (A. and C. Black, 1997)
Radio Drama, Tim Crook (Routledge, 1999)
Radio Drama, Ian Rodger (Macmillan Press, 1982).
Radio Plays: An Epiphanous Use of the Microphone, Beef, Ploughboy Monday, Flos, Kitty Wilkinson, Under the Table, David Pownall (Oberon, 1998)
A Radio Romance, Garrison Keillor (Faber, 1991)

Spoonface Steinbec, I Luv U Jimmy Spud and Other Plays, Lee Hall (BBC books, 1997)

Squirrel's Cage and Other Microphone Plays Tyrone Guthrie (Cobden & Sanderson, 1931)

The Stuff of Radio Lance Sieveking (Cassell, 1934)

Understanding Media, Marshall McLuhan (MIT Press, 1995)

The Way To Write Radio Drama, William Ash (Elm Tree Books, 1985)

Whose is the Kingdom: nine part radio series, John Arden (Methuen, 1988)

Writing For Radio, Colin Haydn Evans (Allison & Busby 1991)

Writing For Radio. Rosemary Horstmann, (A&C Black. 3rd edition 1997) Contains script of *This Gun In My Right Hand Is Loaded* by Timothy West

Writing for Radio, Vincent McInerney, (Manchester University Press, 2001)

Used in the text

www.audiotheater.com/

Discovering the Art of Wireless by Tina Pepler (unpublished thesis)

The Hitch Hiker's Guide to the Galaxy by Douglas Adams, Copyright Serious Productions Ltd 1979 reprinted by permission of Pan Books.

A Suffolk Trilogy, Carey Harrison (Daedelus Press, 1982)

This Gun in my Right Hand is Loaded, Timothy West (A & C Black, 3rd Edition, 1997)

The Vernacular Republic, Poems 1961-1981, Les A. Murray (Angus & Robertson).

Visions by Michio Kaku, (OUP, 1998)

http://home.sprynet.com/~palermo/mtr_radi.htm

Recommended Websites

UK: www.bbc.co.uk/writersroom
       www.irdp.co.uk
       www.oneword.co.uk
       www.soundplay.co.uk

USA: www.home.achilles.net/~jgreen/links.html
       www.home.sprynet.com/~palermo/mtr_radi.htm
       www.greatnorthernaudio.com
       www.audiotheater.com

Index